THE JOY OF PLAYING WITH YOUR DOG

THE **JOY** OF **PLAYING** WITH **YOUR DOG**

Games, Tricks & Socialization
for Puppies & Dogs

THE MONKS OF NEW SKETE
AND
MARC GOLDBERG

PHOTOGRAPHY BY VINCENT REMINI

Countryman Press

An Imprint of W. W. Norton & Company
Celebrating a Century of Independent Publishing

Walking your dog on uneven terrain, using equipment, or interacting with one or more dogs all carry inherent risks to both you and your dog that are impossible to estimate or prevent through any general information resource like this book. Use your own discretion to avoid injury to you or your dog.

For information about permission to reproduce selections from this book, write to Permissions, Countryman Press, 500 Fifth Avenue, New York, NY 10110

For information about special discounts for bulk purchases, please contact W. W. Norton Special Sales at specialsales@wwnorton.com or 800-233-4830

Manufacturing by Versa Press

Countryman Press
www.countrymanpress.com

An imprint of W. W. Norton & Company, Inc.
500 Fifth Avenue, New York, NY 10110
www.wwnorton.com

978-1-68268-504-4

10 9 8 7 6 5 4 3 2 1

To the loving memory of my parents, who shared with
me their passion for life and their love of dogs.
BROTHER CHRISTOPHER

For my beautiful grandchildren, Oliver Davis
Meade and Penelope Opal Meade.
MARC GOLDBERG

CONTENTS

Brother Christopher shares a moment with New Skete German Shepherd puppies.

INTRODUCTION

A pair of bearded men wearing sandals and black robes cinched at the waist strides across a field, their gaze directed downward at a gaggle of puppies playing at their feet. They are on hilly land, but the men keep to a patch of level ground. In the background, a cluster of golden onion domes perch atop a wooden church. Beyond that, the property sits on a mountain that continues to rise several hundred feet, the top covered in a thick pine forest.

At first, they may appear stern, but, at second glance, you'll notice they are merely focusing on the dogs, as they entice the pups to follow them. These men are monks of New Skete, and they are not stern at all. They tread carefully because puppies tend to get underfoot.

The Monks of New Skete live in a secluded Orthodox monastery in Cambridge, New York, 2 miles from the Vermont border. The two monks in the front yard play follow the leader with four 6-week-old German shepherd puppies from a recent litter. The pups follow the monks' encouraging hand claps and jingling keys, keeping the pups moving forward and inter-ested in the game. From time to time, the monks stop and allow the puppies to catch up. As pups often do, they jump at the monks' pant legs for attention. One of the monks picks up a pup and snuggles it close to his face as he speaks in a high-toned voice and is rewarded with a brief puppy-scented lick. He then

puts the pup down and continues the game. Meanwhile, the other monk is already encouraging his puppy to climb a small bank of stairs at the edge of the lawn. After a few minutes of this purposeful playtime, they head back toward the puppy kennel where they started.

Such a game is not an uncommon sight at the monastery. At this monastery founded in 1966, the Monks of New Skete have been breeding German shepherd dogs since the late 1960s and over the years have acquired a reputation for breeding handsome, healthy, and well-socialized dogs. They also train dogs of all breeds at their training facility and have authored two *New York Times* best-selling dog training books, *How to Be Your Dog's Best Friend* and *The Art of Raising a Puppy*. They were featured on a program developed by Animal Planet called *Divine Canine* and, more recently, they collaborated with their friend, author and renowned trainer Marc Goldberg, in writing two new books, *Let Dogs Be Dogs* (2017) and *The Art of Training Your Dog* (2020).

In this current book, *The Joy of Playing with Your Dog*, we share how important it is to provide dogs with a variety of early experiences that are both fun and educational, that promote their growth and development. At the heart of this process is the vital role of play, which seems hardwired into the pups' DNA as soon as they are old enough to see and hear and interact with each other. It is amazing to watch a five-week-old puppy already playing keep-away with one of her littermates, playfully taunting him while holding a soft toy in her mouth, turning away quickly as soon as the other goes for it. Then she struts away several feet and stops, waiting for her littermate to make another attempt. This time the other pup approaches a little more slowly, then suddenly grabs part of the toy, and a spontaneous game of tug-of-war ensues. Meanwhile, two other pups in the litter are on the other side of the pen, "wrestling" with each other, with one pup standing over the other one while the latter is on his back. High-pitched vocalizations arise from both of them as they play out a mock ritual fight. But it's ritualized—it's quite evident that they're having a blast, and suddenly the pup on the bottom manages to right itself and push back into the other, who quickly goes onto *his* back. These spontaneous games ebb and flow throughout the day, interspersed with feeding and nap times.

Puppies learn social interaction through games that will benefit them even as they grow up.

The games will continue throughout the ensuing weeks, until the puppies go to their new homes and families.

Puppies sometimes entice their mothers to play with them, even though a mother may not normally play with other dogs her own age. Puppies can be hard to resist. But when you observe carefully, the mother dog will use playful opportunities to educate her babies. Pups can and do learn many lessons from her, not the least of which is to control the pressure of their bites to keep them gentle. Thus, they learn to control bite pressure with what will eventually be a mouthful of 42 teeth. When to advance and when to yield are also critical lessons mothers teach puppies. Play is not only an important bonding ritual between dogs, but it also offers humans teachable moments during which we can instruct our dogs on skills that will be critical for their well-being and for our overall relationship. Good play, play that serves to build the relationship, is purposeful. Conversely, an inability to play can indicate anxiety or other problems.

At face value, it may not seem apparent how important these interactions are to the social education of young puppies. But on closer examination, they reveal how much growth and development occur in the context of play, both with their littermates and with people. In fact, when such interactions are missing or truncated, for example if the puppies are separated too soon from the mother and litter, the behavioral impact can be serious. Not only does play engage puppies in activity that is fun and appealing, but it also has enormous value in their behavioral development, laying the foundation for a lifetime of quality companionship with their human owners. Wise breeders know this, understanding from experience how important it is to expose puppies to a variety of playful activities during the time they are in their care. This will include play with other dogs, whether littermates or their mother, for example, but also play with human beings.

New Skete's puppy kennel also keeps tunnels and puppy jungle gyms in their pens for the pups to play in and on throughout the day. It is an enriched environment that helps them grow and adjust while having fun. And here is the key: in each context, play will manifest itself in a unique way. For example, pups playing with each other will naturally use their mouths in a way that's appropriate, and that teaches them how to moderate the force of their bite. However, it would be best to avoid this when playing with a human being because we don't want them mouthing us or our children. Instead, redirecting their attention with a line that is attached to a toy can be a positive way of getting them to express their prey drive. But what is common in both situations is the totally engaging activity that is play.

As trainers over many years, Brother Christopher and Marc have seen how crucial a component play is to creating a dynamic relationship with a dog of any age. We remember one man, a successful business executive named George, who adopted a feisty German shepherd he named Ella. He brought the dog to New Skete for training. She was a nice dog, quite sociable, with some preliminary obedience training under her belt. However, when George dropped Ella off with us, he complained that it was difficult to get his dog to settle down.

Ella endlessly demanded attention. When we asked him how much exercise the dog was getting each day, George replied, "I take her on two long walks each day and, since I live and work in New York City, I also have a dog walker take her for an additional walk for an hour in the middle of the day. I've tried my best to train her, and she's pretty good about walking nicely on the leash, but she's just so demanding. When I get home from work, I'm often pretty beat, and doing the second walk is a chore that I know I have to do, but honestly part of me wishes that I could skip it. I don't, but even after the walk it's like she's just getting warmed up."

We asked him what sort of play he did with his dog, and he looked at us quizzically.

"Play? I really don't play with Ella; I just don't have the time."

We explained that it seemed Ella wanted to engage more with him and that he wasn't interpreting the dog's signals properly. It wasn't that Ella was a bad dog—there were no serious behavioral issues—she just needed to be handled more wisely, providing her with both the structure and exercise she was craving. We also assured him it would be possible to integrate play into his life with Ella without having to invest more time that he didn't have. During the following few weeks in our board-and-train program, we refined the obedience exercises that Ella knew and allowed her to play with another training dog who was very friendly. But we also taught Ella to fetch a ball, starting with short tosses wearing a long leash for control, then working up gradually to throwing farther. She took to the game like a duck to water, but what was particularly noticeable was how engaged and joyful she was in the play. It was as if some deep need within her had a new outlet and her face lit up every time that she recognized we were going to play the game.

At the conclusion of Ella's training program, George came to pick her up and to be coached on how to maintain the training. While he watched through a one-way window, Ella easily cruised through her obedience exercises. But what really caught his attention was a demonstration of how she had learned the game of fetch. By now, the dog had learned the rules of the game. Happy with anticipation, she held a sit as we prepared to throw and release her to run down the ball. Off like a

A 15- or 20-foot leash helps prevent the dog from running away with the ball when first learning the game.

Let go of the line when throwing far but pick it up again if needed to guide your dog.

shot, Ella promptly returned to her trainer and sat on command, easily releasing the ball when requested.

As we went through about four long retrieves, George watched through the window, and suddenly a tear ran down the side of his face. Embarrassed, he brushed it aside but he remarked, shaking his head, "This totally blows me away! It just never occurred to me that I could have this kind of fun with Ella at the same time as I'm tiring her out. Amazing! Do you think I could try this while you watch me?" We assured him that this would be entirely possible, and toward the end of our time together we coached him on how to continue working on fetch, complete with the rules that make it productive. It was a joy to get an email several weeks later with a video attachment. It was a 3-minute clip of George playing fetch with Ella, complete with the same joyous enthusiasm, but now with the owner's happy encouragement accompanying the game. Ella ended every play session happily rolling on the ground, delighted, still holding her ball. We could hear George praising her in the background.

That illustrates an important point: play isn't for dogs alone. People need to play, as well. It's vital to our psychological health. In our modern, always-connected society we get a subtle (sometimes even not-so-subtle) message that play is solely for kids, or in this context, dogs. We feel we have to apologize for wanting to do something fun that falls under the umbrella of play. After all, grown-ups should dedicate their time and effort into practical pursuits such as supporting a family, earning a living, making enough money to take care of the needs of our children, saving for their education, and so on. It's a question of being responsible. Of course, these are important concerns, but we also recognize how easy it is to get out of balance, when our energy is so invested in the practical that we neglect activities that re-energize us, that create a renewed sense of enthusiasm and vitality to help us stay faithful to our commitments. Play has a necessary role here.

Yet we are so busy that we have largely forgotten how to play. The lack of play will inevitably take a toll on us. Psychologists counsel that play in its myriad varieties—whether through sports, artwork, games, puzzles—relieves stress, improves brain function, helps stimulate the mind, and boosts creativity. When everything in life

has become so serious, then it is time for us to step back and realign. Playing with your dog can be a very healthy way to do this.

We speak from decades of experience working with dogs and their owners. Brother Christopher has been a member of the Monks of New Skete since 1981 and has been the director of dog training since 1982. Over many years the monks have refined a program that addresses the whole dog, creating a learning environment that is both instructive and fun. They then teach owners how to follow through once their trained dogs return home. In recognition of the contribution the Monks of New Skete have made to the dog training world, the International Association of Canine Professionals (IACP) inducted them into their International Hall of Fame in 2006.

Marc Goldberg has been training dogs since he was 11 years old, when his mother enrolled him and his dog Gus in an obedience training class after Gus had been hit by a car. That initial experience fired a passion in him. Marc joined the Philadelphia Dog Training Club as a young teen. He went from winning obedience competitions to teaching dog training classes in college to working with private clients and their dogs. Marc now runs his own highly successful board-and-train at his Little Dog Farm outside Chicago. Along the way, he has written many training articles and has been the President of the IACP. He was inducted into their members Hall of Fame in 2014. It was a fortuitous meeting between Marc and Brother Christopher at an IACP conference that began a friendship that has only grown stronger over the years.

Having the opportunity to share with each other our insights into all things dog, we realized not only how much we had in common but also recognized a growing desire to collaborate on training seminars as well as books. As already noted, we coauthored *Let Dogs Be Dogs* and followed up with *The Art of Training Your Dog*. We intend this new book to open your mind to a new reality: that, when done in a specific manner, play can not only be joyful but it can also be educational for your dog, leading to better behavior. Trust us when we say that better behavior and more productive time dedicated to your dog will not only make him happy, but it will make you happy too.

———

Dogs are creatures of play who use it to engage with one another and with us to celebrate life. Can we not learn from them? Indeed we can and, if we do, they will teach us to destress, to relax, to take ourselves less seriously, and to enjoy life more. While it is true that they also manifest serious adult behavior in hunting, guarding, or various forms of work, there is always the link with play that provided a natural foundation from their earliest days. So, we invite you to come with us as we explore how to use play as a vital tool to transform your relationship with your dog. For that is what most owners dream of: a relationship that brings out the best in both dogs and ourselves, and that is a joy to experience.

However, productive play—play with a purpose—is vastly different from what so many people actually do with their dogs. Many dogs just get riled up when playing and may leap at their owners, nip, run away, or steal the toys and chew them up. Although *they* may find that fun, you won't find it rewarding. So, you'll probably cut the session short, and you might not want to do it again. But as we said, all good games have rules. Just as organized and well-coached sports can teach many beneficial lessons to children, the same can be said for organized and well-coached play for dogs. You and your dog form a team with you as the coach. You might not need a clipboard and a whistle. But some guidelines and strategies will help you motivate your dog to have a blast while simultaneously learning critical skills such as coming when called, self-calming, and draining energy in a way that will make you both happy. Doesn't that beat the activities your dog may engage in without good coaching? Digging up the yard, barking down the house, and chasing the cat may be on your dog's scorecard right now. But take this journey with us and we know you'll find a better way to get the behavior and relationship you're really looking for.

When you witness a dog and owner playing together with focus, totally in the moment, you don't have to ask what sort of a relationship they have. It is on display before your very eyes. Both of us know this in our bones, and throughout this book, we will share our perspective with you and teach you how to make it work for both you and your dog. Yet aside from our own experience, it is helpful to know that a number of recent behavioral studies on dogs have confirmed the importance of play in the development of happier, healthier, more well-adjusted, and balanced dogs. A convenient source for a number of these studies originally appeared in *The Bark* magazine and are still accessible online.[1] A more detailed book entitled *Canine Play Behavior: The Science of Dogs at Play*[2] provides the most recent scientific evidence on the importance and benefits of play in canine behavior. In short, play with a purpose is fun and it leads you to a better life with your dog.

---

1   Accessible at thebark.com/content/four-scientific-studies-dogs-and-play.
2   Käufer, Mechtilde. *Canine Play Behavior: The Science of Dogs at Play* (Dogwise Publication, 2014).

CHAPTER 1

Instinct: Drives and How They Influence Play

Humanity plays. We have probably done so since before recorded history. The first signs of a formal game were found in Europe and date back 7,000 years to the Bronze Age. But we imagine that well before then, in the 200,000-year history of Homo sapiens, people played all manner of games to pass time, to bond and to hone their skills.

Dogs were domesticated from wolves in Europe and Asia about 30,000 years ago. We suspect that a great deal of time passed before they were brought into homes as members of the family. For a very, very long time it is likely they were more useful as garbage disposals and intruder alarms than as playmates. But surely somewhere along the way, a little girl or boy and a puppy found a commonality expressed in playfulness.

In modern times, we all play games. As children we run off excess energy and make friends through activities like tag and hide and go seek. More organized games come as we get older. We may start with baseball, soccer, lacrosse, or other sports. Getting older, we might take up golf or even card games. From chess to video games, play is for everyone, and the varieties are endless. Human beings are hardwired to spend certain amounts of time playing, and it is easy to see why. Diversion reduces stress and enriches our experience of life.

Interestingly, the same can be said for dogs. Observers of canine behavior note how creative dogs are in engaging in play, even from their earliest weeks. Instincts have a key role here, expressing themselves naturally within the behavior of the litter. For example, two pups manifest what is called pack drive by wrestling play-

Dogs and people express creativity through play.

fully in the yard. It is entirely good-natured and helps them learn how to use their mouths appropriately. Or take the example of a puppy chasing after a blowing leaf in the exercise yard. The leaf triggers the pup's prey drive as the pup tries to pounce on the moving leaf as the wind moves it away. The lesson is clear: from play puppies learn how to interact with the world and, as they mature, play leads them to progressively more adult behaviors that determine their place in the pack. Before domestication, play even influenced survival. You'll see very young puppies engage in stalking behavior (prey drive) and mock combat with one another (defense drive), which eventually would have prepared them to hunt for food and protect their territory. It also helped to reinforce pack cohesion by interacting playfully and regularly with each other. Within the litter, and later within the pack, early dogs played in ways that helped them become a successful species. They honed their skills, built relationships, and determined who among them were the most committed to winning. And while in our day dogs don't have to hunt and defend as they did in the past, these predispositions still express themselves and need to be redirected in healthy ways. They are deeply instinctive.

Yet built into play and all the games that we—and dogs—participate in are rules that govern how the instincts are expressed. All productive games have rules, especially for dogs because they have fast reflexes and 42 teeth. The rules of each game are important. They outline how the play is meant to happen. When players follow the rules, play transpires smoothly, in a positive manner that benefits all

Successful play between dogs, even those who just met, is ritualized to prevent misunderstandings . . . and fights.

participants. Usually, the dogs themselves understand these rules based on instinctual social conventions that they share. But not always. That's why we want you to understand instincts that drive play, and the way one dog will interpret another. Two dogs who go on numerous walks together before finally being turned loose to play will probably have worked out the initial nuances of their relationship because they will have seen one another multiple times. They can begin play with a sense of familiarity that will require less posturing than if the first meeting goes instantly to high-energy interaction. Although this often works out just fine, you'll have more influence over the outcome if you control the introductions. Yes, dogs will instinctively want to play, but for the best chance of a good outcome, knowledgeable owners approach dog socialization with a plan. We'll help you with that in Chapter 10, Socializing Dogs So They Can Play Together. But the important insight is that we have a key role to play in guiding our dogs' instinctive drives toward their flourishing. It doesn't just happen automatically.

Which is why we like to say all good games have rules. This applies to your relationship with your dog as much as it does to human activities such as sports and other games. The value of playing by the rules is that it teaches self-discipline and teamwork. It keeps both parties in bounds while helping us mature as we enjoy the process of becoming more bonded and more skilled in our interactions. Think of athletes on a team who practice long and hard through a season and eventually win a championship. They don't achieve this by cheating on the rules. Rather, they strive to play within the rules of the game and the relationships they forge through that process often last a lifetime. We have an opportunity to teach critical concepts to our dogs, including the most important skill of all: impulse control, the ability to respond to her owner when distracted instead of ignoring and simply doing her own thing. When you successfully take the time to teach your dog how to play the games in this book, you build the relationship. At the same time your dog learns to be more responsive to your needs. Teaching him to control his instinctive impulses while he has fun has a hugely beneficial effect on the relationship.

On the other hand, if we don't clarify rules and boundaries for a dog, the results will be undesirable, accidentally reinforcing unwanted dog behaviors while increasing your own frustration. Take the example of fetch. Many dogs love it because it goes to the heart of their prey drive. Say your dog gets super excited when you grab the ball and head for the door. As you move you feel the dog jumping persistently at your backside, wild with anticipation. Instead of pausing until the behavior ceases— essentially saying we don't play until you move with me calmly—you try to get the dog out the door and into the yard quickly. You'll discover that the dog's jumping behavior will be even more frenzied, and she will tend to express that in similar situations when she gets excited. It may even escalate into spinning and barking. Next thing you know, you're frustrated and yelling NO. Now both *you* and the dog are barking! And the relationship is affected. On the other hand, if your dog can control her excitement and walk happily but politely into the yard, you'll both feel better. She will be practicing impulse control to get to the fun bit, and that will carry over naturally into other areas of her life.

Instinct influences behavior, but so do emotion and desire. As important as instincts are in canine development and flourishing, they are not the whole story. Dogs are not robotically instinctive. They are creatures with emotions that blend with their instincts to actively seek what is good in their environment. Dr. Temple Grandin, the famous animal behaviorist, in her book *Animals Make Us Human*, shows convincingly how this seeking behavior positively affects the lives of all

We share a desire to play, plus a range of emotions, with our dogs.

animals. By using her insights, when we apply seeking behavior to the instinctive life of dogs, we find that dogs naturally engage in play because it generates positive emotions: when the seeking system is triggered in the brain it causes them to move forward, sniff, explore their environment and interact with other members of their species as well as humans. This naturally leads to play behaviors they find pleasurable. Little wonder. People and dogs both seek pleasure. Some of what makes us feel emotionally good is common between the species. We both delight in a cuddle or close proximity at the end of a busy day. And at other points we will diverge. The dog will take pleasure from indulging his instinct to cover his own scent by rolling in the sort of smell and substance that we would rather avoid altogether. Although the psychological study of dogs lags far behind that of humans, does any dog owner doubt their dog feels emotions such as joy, worry or contentment? Then there is our innate ability to read one another's intentions. When walking your dog, you know what he's going to bark or alert at, often before he does it. And if you accidentally step on his foot, when he yelps causing you to apologize instantly, notice how quickly and obviously he forgives you. Compare that with a time you scolded him, and he seemed glum for far longer than when you accidentally but physically trod on him.

We believe the difference in his emotional reactions is the sincere apology you

Play bonds us closely, like teammates.

made. He probably didn't understand the words, but he read your tone of voice and loving touch to signify *I didn't mean it*. Tens of thousands of years of togetherness have affected both species. Our long history with dogs coupled with their guileless nature enables us to look at much of their body language and easily interpret it. You don't have to take an animal sciences class to recognize a puppy's play bow as an invitation. Similarly, we humans have so affected the dog's evolution through selective breeding that they can tell when we are happy with them or not. Even though the dog may know when we don't approve of his behavior that doesn't mean he understands what we want him to do instead. And being uneducated, he may well focus more on pleasing himself than his owner. The playful nature of the dog, emanating from a combination of instinct and emotion, gives us an opening, an opportunity to trade him better behavior as we define it in return for the attention and activities that he craves. Specifically, as it relates to play and building a close relationship with our dog, we can harness the dog's primary instincts of pack drive and prey drive to make this happen in a way the dog loves.

As trainers, we have both learned valuable lessons about dogs and their behavior by the mistakes we have made. Reflecting on his early days as a trainer, Marc offers a pertinent and illuminating example of what he learned from his first dog, Gus: "Much of what I know about them, I've learned directly from dogs. If you've read my previous books, you know that this began with a Sheltie named Gus, the first dog I would come to love. He was a gift for my 11th birthday. Although we enrolled in obedience school because he had been tumbled by a car, working together soon became something more than a safety measure. We relished one another's company. I loved spending time with my dog, and I was fascinated at how quickly he learned anything I tried to teach him.

After winning first prize in beginner's obedience class, I began to train Gus more intensively so we could compete in the American Kennel Club contests, which were very popular then. We developed a routine. I'd come home from school, take Gus outside, and play with him. Sometimes I threw his ball. Other times I just grabbed an apple off our massive tree and threw that for him until it got chewed up and slobbery. Then I would sit down on the ground, pat my leg and my best friend would hop onto my lap for some petting. The whole process only took 5 or 10 minutes, but it was a fun habit. After a short rest we would then begin training lessons.

Gus and I began to win prizes at the dog shows. He was a very smart little fellow and we won piles of silver platters and trophies that I still have to this day. By now I was 12 or 13 and winning started to feel good. Our names appeared in the *Philadelphia Inquirer*'s dog show column and I entered Gus in more shows. It made me ambitious.

One Friday I came home from school and remembered that the next day we would be competing. I changed my clothes in a rush, snapped a leash on Gus, and hustled him outside to practice. But something was wrong. Gus would not work for me. Instead, he did something he had never done before: he flat out refused to budge. I stopped trying to train him and I began to think. Something was different, something was wrong, but what? That's when it struck me that I had broken our pattern of play first, train second. But could that really be the reason my always willing dog stubbornly quit on me?

I sat down on the ground, patted my leg and, after a brief pause, Gus hopped into my lap. I loved on him for a while, then pitched an apple. He brought it back and I threw it again. A moment later I put the leash back on and Gus happily worked for me. Perhaps it's my imagination clouded by the 50 years that have passed since that day, but I would swear he had a slightly triumphant look on his face, as though Gus was satisfied to have taught *me* a lesson.

The next day we won another silver plate. A bit tarnished and dusty, it now rests on an upper bookshelf in my den. But the lesson he taught me that day was the far more valuable prize. You see, Gus worked for me because he loved me and because he knew I wanted him to. Playing with him was the way I returned the love. It was baked into our social contract.

Thinking back to my time with Gus, I realize that our play paid dividends with good behavior. The dog who ran away and was smacked by a car became the dog who fetched whatever I threw for him. He accompanied me to local tennis courts and ran down my wild lobs. It was nearly impossible to play hide and go seek with my sister and friends because Gus always knew which closet I was hiding in, and he sat at its door waiting for me. I was always the first to be found.

He learned to bark on command when I said *speak* and that helped us in two ways. First, he quit barking for no reason—and if you've ever had a Sheltie, you know they're a charming but very barky breed. And second, when he did bark down the house in the middle of one autumn night, I paid attention to him and found our back door jimmied open. Undoubtedly Gus saved us from a burglary or worse that night.

Had I trained Gus without playing games with him, ours would have been a mechanical relationship, composed of technical accomplishments, but certainly not the rich and full life we gave one another. Gus taught me that through playing games we can share love and lessons at the same time."

And as we will teach you in this book, all good games have rules. Learning to abide by the rules will help your dog have fun while learning to become a safer and happier pet.

This points to the fact that play and learning are interrelated. Both involve assimilating information and following rules that give direction to their instincts. Dogs who play well, with their owners and with other dogs, have often been properly prepared. You will have a more predictable path to enjoyment in your relationship with your dog through the sort of purposeful play we will guide you to in this book. We will take you through many options of structured play that are age-appropriate, and that will allow you and your dog to reach a level of mutual enjoyment that should last throughout his life. We'll cover puppies, moving into games for adolescents, then adult dogs and finally seniors. We have written several books about how to formally train your dog and we strongly believe in its value. But we are also realistic, so we understand that you will spend far more time living and playing with your dog than

Dogs are social animals. Many enjoy the company of their own kind.

formally training him. That is precisely why we've hidden some crucial behavior improvements within the games and play that follow.

Play can be structured or unstructured. Structured play is intentional and purposeful. It capitalizes on your dog's instincts by *teaching* her, using skills your dog knows, or is learning, and strengthens those skills as your dog enjoys activities with you. Your dog learns to follow the rules of the game, and the hidden benefit is that it strengthens your relationship. Unstructured play is less intentional and while forms of it can be beneficial for your dog (such as playing with other dogs at day care), there's also a greater chance for problems to arise. Often these occur in unintentional ways that reinforce unwanted behavior. We recall a client whose Vizsla, Jenny, had a real problem with jumping up on people. They brought the dog to us after Jenny knocked over the wife's elderly mother during a visit. Fortunately, the mother wasn't badly hurt, but they couldn't afford to have it happen again. As they got Jenny out of the car, the 10-year-old son held a toy over his head to excitedly play with her. Jenny began jumping wildly, trying to grab it as the boy shrieked in delight.

The Vizsla is a hunting breed, a Hungarian bird dog who points and retrieves

Dogs may try to play games that they like but that we do not.

game. So, Jenny was a hunting dog, and like all dogs, she had an instinct for hunting baked into her DNA. Broadly speaking, we'll call this instinct "prey drive." This is the drive to chase and catch prey. She is hard wired to want it. That toy, dangling just out of reach, pushed her prey drive button, but not in the purposefully structured way a hunter would have done. Of course, a 10-year-old boy wouldn't automatically know better but he invented a game that both he and Jenny loved, but which strengthened the wrong behavior. Watching the scene, the husband said dryly, "So this is what we're dealing with." It was a classic example of play without rules that had accidentally become dangerous.

And that leads us to remind you that not all play is helpful. For example, a dog who constantly tries to grab the leash away from you is playing a game that will not contribute to cooperation. But it is undeniable that dogs like to tug, so later in this book we will teach you a safe and effective way to play the game so it will lead to both better behavior and a better relationship.

You see, the prey drive we discussed is the instinct underlying much of dog play. It has a lot to do with why even very young puppies stalk, chase, and pounce. But the other primary instinct "pack drive" can be defined as the dog's instinctual need for companionship, coupled with his desire to please. He recognizes and responds positively to a nuanced hierarchy. After all, the dog is a social animal, meant to live with others, with his pack, whether it be entirely a human pack plus himself or with people and other dogs in the family unit. In 1978, the Monks coined a new term to describe the role of the dog owner, so we might better explain our instinctive importance to the dog.

That term is "pack leader."

It has a storied history. It was first used in studies on wolves to describe pack hierarchy and dynamics. The Monks then applied the concept to the human/dog relationship in *How to be Your Dog's Best Friend.* Their second book, *The Art of Raising a Puppy,* went into more detail on what it means to be a good Pack Leader. Together the Monks and Marc wrote *Let Dogs Be Dogs* in 2017 to put a fine point on all the ways a good Pack Leader lives with a dog. Then, in 2020 we wrote *The Art of Training Your Dog to* detail how a good Pack Leader trains the dog.

In this book, we will show you how to play with your dog—for better behavior of course. We have tried to cover the full and rich spectrum of the best ways to love and raise a dog. How to live with the dog. How to train the dog. How to play with the dog. It all works because although the dog has prey drive, he is also a social animal. The dog's natural pack drive allows him not only to enjoy play but also to follow the rules we'll incorporate. That's why we are always mindful that all good games have rules and a good Pack Leader, like a good coach, brings out the best in his or her team.

Brother Christopher, mother dog, and puppies play Follow the Leader.

CHAPTER 2

Benefits of Structured Play and Rules to Improve Behavior

All of us know the experience of playing games. As children, we play everything from hopscotch to hide and go seek, to more organized games as we get older, from little league and midget football to soccer, tennis, and golf. Play is for everyone, and the varieties are endless. Human beings are hardwired to spend a certain amount of time playing and it is easy to see why: play enriches our experience of life. Interestingly, the same holds true for dogs. Observers of canine behavior note how creative dogs are in engaging in play, even from their earliest weeks. Dogs use play to learn how to interact with the world and as dogs mature, play leads them to progressively more adult behaviors that determine their survival. Before domestication, for example, that meant hunting for food and protecting their territory. It also meant reinforcing pack cohesion by interacting playfully and regularly with each other. And while modern dogs don't have to hunt and defend as they did in the past, nevertheless these impulses still express themselves and need to be redirected in healthy ways. They are deeply instinctive.

Yet built into play and all the games that we participate in are rules that are important to follow. Rules outline how the play is meant to happen. When the players follow the rules, the play transpires smoothly, in a positive manner that everyone enjoys. Let's imagine how this might work out. Your best friend

has a goldendoodle who loves to play and who has become good friends with your labradoodle. They have known each other for a short while. They were introduced first by taking walks together and then by playing together in your fenced-in backyard. They now have regular playdates a couple of times a week in which the dogs play happily in the backyard, good-naturedly jousting and mouthing each other and then sprinting into a spontaneous version of tag as you and your friend catch up on the patio, drinking iced tea. The dogs are able to play energetically for quite some time, and by the end of visiting with your friend, they are pretty much gassed.

But let's imagine another scenario, this one a bit darker. Suppose the dogs don't really know each other all that well and you and your friend simply assume that they will play appropriately. You watch them interact a bit tentatively at first, jumping

Because some are too competitive, dogs should know each other well before you let them play with toys together.

around, then freezing, then putting their mouths on each other. But as they grow more and more excited, the play becomes rougher and rougher and quickly starts to spiral out of control. One dog nips the other a bit too forcefully, and before you know it, the two of them are genuinely angry at each other and have to be separated before it escalates into a full-blown dog fight. How did things go south so quickly?

The simplest explanation is that the dogs didn't really understand the rules. In the first scenario, the dogs had been trained to understand the nature of the game they were playing. The owners had taken the time to let the dogs know each other and from there, they were able to guide them in their play with each other. In the second

Dogs who already know each other can meet up like old friends.

example, the approach was more of a spontaneous throw of the dice. There was no real preparation, no teaching of the rules of the game, just the presumption that the dogs would instinctively know how to play with each other. For some dogs, that may work out, but for the vast majority it is going to be a real gamble that can result in chaos. We'll talk a lot more about socializing dogs so they can play together safely in Chapter 10 (page 177).

All good games have rules that the participants must follow. This applies to our relationship with our dogs as much as it does to human activities such as sports and other games. The value of playing by the rules is that it teaches self-discipline and teamwork. It helps us mature while at the same time letting us enjoy the process of becoming more and more skilled in an activity. Think of athletes on a team who practice long and hard through a season and eventually win a championship. They don't achieve this by cheating on the rules. Rather, they strive to play within the rules of the game, and the relationships they forge through that process often last a lifetime. With dogs, games have the opportunity to teach impulse control, the ability to respond to her owner when distracted instead of ignoring her, and simply doing her own thing.

Impulse control is critical for dogs, and for people too for that matter. We cannot do everything that occurs to us simply because we want to. For example, at a buffet we do not push people out of the way to grab handfuls of food right out of the tray. We might *want* to, but we don't. That's impulse control. In traffic, we might want to lean on the horn and scream out the window but we control the impulse.

Of course, we weren't born with impulse control. When very young we *do* try to grab anything we want. And we don't ask. As 2-year-olds, our parents constantly intercepted our hands, reminding us to say *please* and *thank you* rather than *gimme* and grabbing. By the time a 2-year-old child reaches the age of 4 or 5, that education begins to kick in. The "terrible 2s" are over and, although parenting doesn't end, some important impulse control skills have been well started. Eventually, as adults we won't depend entirely upon external reminders to control our impulses and mind our manners. We begin to tap the figurative and literal brakes on our own behavioral impulses. Even so, a single traffic ticket for failing to control an impulse to speed can serve as a long-lasting reminder to be more careful in the future.

Learning impulse control is the single most important benefit of play.

When you successfully teach your dog how to play a game using its set of rules—say fetch—you'll build the relationship at the same time as you teach your dog to be more and more responsive to your commands. You'll teach her to control her impulses at the same time she's having fun. That makes your teaching job and her learning job far easier to accomplish than in any other context. This will have a hugely beneficial effect on your relationship. Imagine a dog who wants to eat the garbage or steal food off the counters but refrains because it's against the rules. That's impulse control at its finest and is precisely what you need from your dog. The best dog is one who thinks, *I could. But I won't.*

If we don't take the time to teach impulse control by clarifying the rules of the game with our dog, the results will be less felicitous. They will likely reinforce irritating and unwanted behavior while increasing your frustration. Take the example of fetch. Say your dog gets super excited when you grab the ball and head for the door. As you move, you feel her jumping persistently at your back, poking, and nudging you, impolite with anticipation. You now have two options.

36 THE JOY OF PLAYING WITH YOUR DOG

First is the correct one, which, although counterintuitive to humans, really works. You can simply freeze in place and wait it out until the behavior ceases. It usually doesn't take more than a minute or two. Once you move, the dog will likely resume jumping so you merely repeat until you can get through the door while the dog controls her impulse to jump on you. That's a profound teachable moment for you and an equally important learning experience for your dog.

Most people will inadvertently choose the second option. They'll loudly scold the dog in frustration while simultaneously moving faster to get outside and begin the game, all in an effort to end the madness. What will the dog learn in this all-too-common instance? *When I frustrate my owner with wild behavior, he'll move faster to give me the rewarding activity.* In simpler terms: crime pays.

This dog exercises great impulse control by waiting for the ball.

You're better off taking extra time to calmly and quietly show your dog that *please* and *thank you* in the form of canine politeness will work much faster than jumping and demanding. The benefits will extend far beyond just that one game of fetch that you intended to play. That moment during which your dog learned that impulse control gets her what she wants quicker than overexcitement has taught her to take a moment to self-calm in order to achieve her objective. You will be amazed and gratified to see how that concept will carry over naturally into other areas of her life.

What this points to is the fact that play and training are interrelated. Both involve learning and following rules so that the dog can ultimately be trusted, earn more liberty, and derive more enjoyment from togetherness with her family. Dogs who play well, whether individually with their owners or more broadly with other dogs, are generally dogs who have been properly trained. The notion that dogs will magically play well without an underlying program of training is fanciful and usually means that the owner doesn't want to take the time to teach their dog. While most of us recognize our dogs need a certain amount of exercise so that they can be easier to live with, some owners try to take a short cut, thinking that all this requires is letting their dogs run free in a dog park for a half hour. Although it works for some, that can be a recipe for problems. Our clients report various issues related to dog parks. These include difficulty calling the dog back when it's time to leave; stealing other dog's toys; or worse yet, getting into scraps with other dogs, whether their dog was the aggressor or the victim. Many of these problems stem from not being taught how to play safely with other dogs. Although we'll discuss that more in Chapter 10 (page 177), it all goes back to structured play that helps your dog learn to modify her behavior—even when she faces temptation—so that the game can continue.

You will have much more success and enjoyment in your relationship with your dog if you accept the fact that dogs need both formal training and structured play. The two work hand in hand. In this book we will guide you through a program of structured play that will allow you and your dog to reach a level of mutual enjoyment that should last throughout his life. Yet this presumes a backdrop of structure that simply means putting rules to the game and reinforcing them.

Play can be structured or unstructured. Structured play is intentional and taught. It teaches a game using skills your dog knows (or is learning) and reinforces those skills as your dog has fun with you doing an activity that appeals to her. She learns to follow the rules of the game while it strengthens your relationship. Unstructured play is less intentional and while forms of it can be beneficial for your dog (such as playing with other dogs at day care), there's also a greater chance for problems to arise. Often these occur in unintentional ways that reinforce unwanted behavior. We recall a couple who brought their young golden retriever to us for basic training. When they arrived for the drop-off, they accidentally let the dog out of the car without a leash. The dog proceeded to play a game of catch-me-if-you-can for the next half-hour, zooming back and forth outside the reach of the frustrated owners. When they finally caught him, the embarrassed husband confessed, "This is exactly why we've brought Auggie here for training. He has absolutely no idea what 'come' means." "On the contrary," we observed, "he knows what it means, he's just learned that he doesn't have to do it." Once again, another classic example of an unintentional game that lacked any rules and that had now become dangerous.

There are types of play that are counterproductive. Apart from unintentional training as in the above example with Auggie, certain games are harmful for dogs and you should never engage in them. For example, we suggest you do not play with your dog and a laser pointer. We know dogs love to chase after moving objects and that this might be a good way to give exercise and wear them out. That is the value of playing fetch. However, some owners apply this principle by using laser pointers to send their dogs into a chase frenzy. At face value it seems harmless enough and the dog seems to enjoy it, running back and forth chasing after the moving red dot. Even better, it tires him out. What's the problem? This overstimulated chase with no capture often triggers obsessive-compulsive behavior or anxiety in dogs who may be prone to it. While dogs do love to chase, normally they are running after an object that they can catch, such as a ball, a frisbee, or a stick. These are positive outlets for their prey drive and boost dogs' self-confidence when they track down whatever they're chasing, preferably in the context of a structured game. It's also great exercise.

The problem with using a laser pointer, however, is that the dog never "wins." They never get the "prey" because the laser pointer is always moving away from them. This can be confusing and frustrating for a dog and can lead to obsessive behavior that is hard to fix because they can get stuck in chase mode. Thus, they begin to chase anything that moves, even shadows and reflective lights, or stare fixedly at where they last saw the red dot, waiting for the prey to reappear. Although it won't affect every dog the same way, the percentages are high enough to concern us. Take this advice seriously: don't mess with a dog's mind by having him chase after a laser pointer.

As we said, dogs love to play tug and it can be an excellent way to release energy.

This boy has been asked to sit briefly and wait for permission to tug.

His patience is rewarded with permission to tug and play.

Before teaching rules, you may get unwanted tugging on your leash as Marc found here.

The dog who learns to take and release the tug on command shows a high degree of impulse control that will translate positively to the overall relationship with the owner. For the dog who never learns to let go, the exact opposite will be the case. These dogs may well develop behavior problems involving resource guarding and possessiveness. They may grab any random object you are holding, even items which you have not designated as a toy. Tug is a game that must be taught in a structured way with very clear rules, and we'll do just that in Chapter 8 (page 135).

Games and the play that makes them both fun and stimulating offer dogs and their owners the chance to bond and deepen their relationships. There is a vast difference between a dog playing fetch with her owner for a half hour, retrieving the ball consistently, releasing it, then waiting patiently for the next toss, versus the dog who wrestles the ball away from his owner, then runs away with it. He tops off the session by eluding the owner's frustrated attempts to leash him. The first example is positive: it reinforces the dog's understanding of appropriate behavior that will carry over into the rest of the day. The second example has no such effect. It will only reinforce the dog's sense of being in control and can easily morph into inappropriate mouthing of humans and failure to come when called because fleeing is more rewarding that coming. The proof is in the pudding: all good games reflect the owner being in control of the game and the dog following the rules.

The happiest dogs have learned that play is a give and take.

CHAPTER 3

Recall Games

*S*it and *stay* and *down* are all useful skills for your dog to know, but the *come* command will save your dog's life. A dog with a reliable recall can be redirected away from potentially dangerous situations involving cars and other animals. One sad statistic shows that as many as a million dogs per year are struck by cars. While this book is intended to bring you and your dog together with the many benefits of purposeful play, this chapter is the real lifesaver.

That's not why we typically use the command, of course. It is not often that our dogs chase a ball or a squirrel toward the street, but we can prepare for this possible emergency well in advance. Even if you always leash walk your dog, what about that one time in a million when the leash accidentally slips through your fingers? Most of the time, we ask dogs to come to us in a quieter and more relaxed situation, such as when we want to get ready for a walk, or we want them to come back inside after going potty in the backyard. But practice for potential emergencies will keep him safer.

Our human tendency to teach and use the *come* command only in these quiet circumstances can lead to problems when we need our dogs to respond when faced with a more urgent situation.

Untrained, a dog only comes to you when he believes it is in his best interest. The dog responds to a call because he might get treats or attention, or he is about to enjoy an activity such as dinner or a walk. Although your dog may come for love, he is still coming to you for some type of personal reward.

Recall games are not only fun but can save your dog's life.

Dogs Are Intelligent, Complex, Problem-Solving, Domesticated Predators

Dogs weigh their options. Much like people, they look at the world through a filter of what is likely to benefit them most. Often, because of your training and because of the love your dog has for you, he will come when you call. It is easy to obey a dinnertime command when nothing more interesting is happening.

But it is far more difficult with distractions present. Think of a time when your dog is loose in the yard, chasing a butterfly or sniffing the ground where a raccoon may have paused during the night. The calculation changes. Your dog does not always know what is best for him. So, when you call out, he may not feel inclined to listen with so many other fun or interesting options competing for his attention. It is one thing to get your dog to listen when nothing else is going on around him. It is quite another when he is surrounded by more interesting distractions.

How many times have you called your dog when he was engrossed in a sniff and thought, "He doesn't even hear me"? In fact, he literally might *not* have heard you. The dog's brain can send all resources to the nose, denying access to the ears. The good news is you can teach him to keep a small part of his mind available to listen for you much the way a small part of your cell phone's circuitry is always listening for you to call upon the virtual assistant.

On the other hand, have you ever been quite sure that your dog heard your call yet didn't respond? Perhaps he briefly paused his sniff across the yard, looked up at you, yet immediately ignored you, returning to his own preferred activity? When this happens you understandably get frustrated, repeat the commands uselessly, and eventually stomp toward the dog to interrupt the distraction.

If we could read the dog's mind at such moments, the thought we'd likely hear is: *Don't be a party pooper!* And from *his* perspective, endowed with powers of observation, hearing and scent so powerful that we cannot fully comprehend them, he's right. We *are* party poopers spoiling the fun. The problem of course is that instinct is a powerful motivator for dogs. And discipline alone is rarely enough to teach a reliable recall in the presence of distractions. In other words, if you don't prepare ahead of time, the moment you most need your dog to recall will inevitably come when he is least inclined to listen to you. So, let's not use discipline alone to teach the *come* command. Let's make it great fun for your dog by harnessing some of his most powerful instincts. This way you can not only practice preparing ahead for an emergency, but you can also have fun together as you help your dog exercise his body and his mind.

To give your dog more practice in learning this skill, we have designed games that teach him how to do the following:

- Reserve some attention for you at all times.
- Find it more rewarding to respond to your calls.
- Connect further with you as the owner, reinforcing the idea that when you call, it's important.

We want to teach your dog that although curiosity is a natural part of his nature, he should also remain aware of you so he will rarely be so distracted that he is unable to hear you.

It is true that practice makes perfect, and never has that been truer than it is with *come when called*. Exciting and happy recall games with your dog will make him safer and protect him from dangers we hope he never has to face. Typically, dogs also find these games very enjoyable, adding to their benefit.

Before We Learn, We Have to Avoid "Unlearning"

As you know, the Monks of New Skete and Marc Goldberg have been training dogs of all breeds since the 1970's. And although this is a book about how to play with a purpose, you didn't think we'd let you get away without a few training tips, did you? One secret we have unlocked is that dogs are *always* learning. Even when we don't actually intend to teach them a lesson, they will learn from our reactions and responses to their behavior. Nowhere is this truer than when teaching a dog to come when called, especially in an emergency situation.

It is vitally important you do not unintentionally teach your dog to ignore the command during your own day-to-day behaviors. Doing so will both make it harder to play these games and make it more difficult to convince your dog to respond to you when he is otherwise occupied. That's why, before we jump into recall games, we want to give you a few ways to make this chapter easier to apply and even more useful.

First, when you are practicing, tone matters. We always want the *come* command to be said in a way that sounds friendly, never angry. Recall always must be associated with an opportunity for good things. Your dog can pick up on an angry or frustrated voice. He knows when he's in trouble just like you did when you heard that certain tone along with your middle name as a child. Calling with an angry voice introduces the likelihood for conflict, which your dog would prefer to avoid.

However, we also want to teach your dog that different tones still have the same meaning and need to be responded to equally.

Much of the time, when we call our dogs at home, we do so in a caring voice. But if your pet is faced with danger, chances are you are not going to call in that same quiet and relaxed tone. You're going to shout out to your dog, making sure he hears you, because you need a quick response.

That is why it is also a good idea to occasionally practice the command—both during these games and on your own—in tones that your dog is likely to hear if faced with danger. We want him to know you may happily call for him with raised volume, and he should still respond because that volume does not indicate that you are angry.

This means that as you introduce games during which your dog will find himself far from you, it is OK to put a bit of urgency in your voice, a higher volume. For example, you can practice when throwing a toy for your dog because he'll run away from you to get it. Calling him back once he has it will remind him about the most important part of this game. Ideally, we want him to bring back the toy, but the most important part of this game is that he comes back when called. Just don't sound angry. At appropriate moments, you can sound both louder than normal *and* happy. Training your dog to respond to a commanding voice in addition to a kind voice is a good idea that will pay off in the long run.

Opposite page: *Fetch is a fun game, but the most important part is the recall when your dog comes back to you even though he is excited.*

Second, never call your dog in a frustrated tone and then punish him.

This requires training *yourself*.

Too often, owners will call a dog to scold him for an infraction such as chewing a shoe or having an accident. To you it may seem natural to call your dog so he can face the music for an unwanted behavior. But for your pet, it is very undoglike behavior to approach an obviously angry member of the pack. His every instinct will be to placate with avoidance. Yet this is the opposite of what you want and will probably frustrate you more.

Repeatedly calling a dog when you are angry will leave a lasting impression, one that can be undone, but only when you take the time and effort to show your dog that you have changed and become more understanding. Dogs are forgiving creatures! Just remember, don't call a dog then reprimand him after he has obeyed the command, one which should have earned him praise.

Equally important is not to inadvertently teach your dog that you will be unpredictable with your hands. Most of the time, you use your hands to pet or give treats and that creates a positive association. But sometimes you may sternly grab forbidden items from your dog's mouth. Or you might abruptly reach for his collar to move him away from something like a hot stove. In fact, we frequently tend to use our hands this way, especially with busybody puppies who get into everything.

That is why we highly recommend, particularly with younger dogs, that you minimize physical grabbing of the dog or collar and avoid harsh tones. It unintentionally teaches the dog not to always come because when you call, your dog may take a moment to evaluate whether he is in trouble and would be better off avoiding you. Always associate coming to you with something pleasant.

Using a Drag Line for a Happier Puppy and Owner

But that doesn't mean you'll let your dog go anywhere or pick up anything he wants. He is bound to get into some shenanigans until he learns the house rules, and you'll need a way to stop him without "unteaching" the recall and without teaching him that your hands are unpredictable.

For this, we recommend using what we call a "drag line."

Drag lines are a dog trainer trick we recommend you use under supervision until your puppy or dog learns your rules for what he can and can't chew, etc. Rather than angrily calling your dog to prevent him from getting into trouble, you can simply step on the line, stopping him from going into a forbidden area. Then you can bend down, extend a treat, and use this opportunity to create a teachable moment for recall. It is especially useful if you have a puppy because they so often do naughty behaviors. If we're not careful, we might spend the first 6 months of their lives chasing them, grabbing things away from them, and scolding. All those things harm the recall you'll need for the rest of his life!

As a side note, when your pup or dog picks up something she shouldn't have, which she inevitably will, don't make a big fuss about it. Step on the drag line so she can't run away, and walk on the line until you are close to your dog. Gently take the item and give her something to replace it, such as a toy you approve of. Problem solved in a way that won't later interfere with teaching recall or fetch.

A drag line is a nylon line or leash, about 10 feet long. Cut any handle off the end so it is less likely to get caught on furniture. The line is allowed to drag, trailing behind the dog. Attach it to a flat collar, not a training collar. When carefully supervised, you can now allow your dog or puppy freedom of movement without having to overuse the recall to interrupt his natural curiosity. Remember, frequently calling your dog to stop him from breaking a house rule will cause your dog to see you as a "spoil-sport," thus making him likely to begin ignoring you.

For example, you see your young dog Gizmo has started to sniff at a kitchen countertop. Most people are going to do at least one of the following: scold him loudly, rush toward him, grab his collar or body, maybe angrily call him to you. Any of those responses will eventually complicate the recall you truly need.

With a dragline, you can quickly and quietly pick up the end of the line and walk your puppy away without a word. It is a safe, gentle technique that takes him away from the situation quickly and calmly. It is also silent, which teaches him the rule holds even when you're not there to scold him.

It is also a great way to train and play.

Drag lines offer a way to both stop your dog from an unwanted behavior and help him learn the desired ones. You can correct your dog when he starts to make a mistake during training, or you can lead him toward the behavior you want. Use the line to take him away from nosing the trash or counters but immediately turn that into an opportunity to guide him into a recall with sit for a treat. This works even for puppies as young as 8 weeks. Throughout the following recall games, a drag line or long leash is a great way to help bring your dog to you without raising your voice or grabbing if he runs the wrong way. For safety, use only while observing, otherwise take it off.

Now that you have your drag line or long leash, it is time to play the first game. Remember, each of these games is meant to help your pet learn to stop what he's doing and come to you when called, no matter how enticing the distraction.

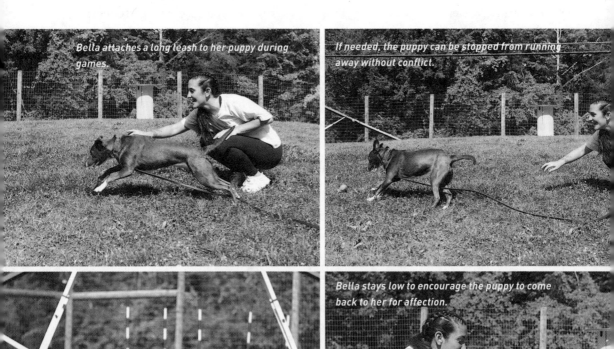

Bella attaches a long leash to her puppy during games.

If needed, the puppy can be stopped from running away without conflict.

Bella stays low to encourage the puppy to come back to her for affection.

Paper Plate Recall

Among trainers, this is a popular game. Marc recalls playing a version of it in the early 1970's with his first dog Gus. You need two different types of treats for this game. One is good, but the other is great. The first is something your dog likes; the second is one he loves. For example, you can use pieces of your dog's kibble as the first type, and a soft training treat for the second. With dogs who need extra motivation, you can use soft training treats as the "good" and small pieces of chicken or string cheese as the "great" treats. You will have the more desirable treat in your pocket, using the lesser one for the first part of the game. If you don't want food in your pocket, clip a treat bag on your clothing for easy access.

With your dog attached to a line stretched out on the ground in front of him, tell him to sit and stay. Then place a paper plate on the ground about 6 feet in front of him. He may want to get up as you do so, but this is your opportunity to remind him that you asked him to remain sitting despite the distraction you are creating. If he should get up, calmly but insistently use the line to guide him back to sit where you originally placed him.

Let your dog watch you put a treat on the plate. Step back to your dog. Then release him from the sit, gesturing toward the plate to indicate that he can run over to eat the treat. If needed, walk to the paper plate, pointing to the treat so he gets the idea.

As he is eating the treat and sniffing the plate to see if he missed any crumbs, quietly step back to your original position. Once you are there, call your dog back to you in a happy, loud tone of voice. After all, you'll probably be interrupting his attempt to find more treats on that plate. If he comes to you readily, immediately offer a *second* treat, this time the "great" one you reserved for this purpose.

What should you do if your dog is so distracted with that paper plate that he can't be bothered to abandon it and come right to you? Resist the temptation to call him again or you'll just teach him to wait for your second or even third command. Instead, pick up the line and reel him in hand over hand without saying a word. Don't be angry or frustrated. You are simply making good use of a teachable moment.

1. Let your dog see the treat without going to it (upper left).

2. Then release him to get the treat (upper right).

3. Eventually you can send him from a farther distance (center right).

4. Call him back and reward him with an even better treat and praise (bottom).

Once you've got your dog close to you, show him the great treat that he could have had. You can even let him lick it, *but don't let him eat it.* Instead, repeat the entire process again right away, giving him an immediate opportunity to earn that special tidbit. Ask him to sit. Place the "good" treat on the plate, send him to it, then call him back same as last time.

Now it is much likelier that he will come right back to you because he knows you have something even better than the paper plate. You have just converted the paper plate into a reward, but also a distraction. And that's crucial because distractions are very rewarding for your dog on an instinctual level. The essence of what we are teaching with this game is this: no matter how rewarding you may find the distraction, I will always be *more* important and *more* rewarding.

Over time, as you repeat the game, increase the distance from you and your sitting dog to the paper plate. As he learns, you might need to use the line to stop him from running to the plate before you release him, but eventually he'll understand he only earns the reward by waiting for permission to go and that you have something even better to offer anyway.

Once you're able to play with the plate 20 to 30 feet away, it is time to add a new step. While holding the leash, tell your dog he can go and get the treat. But before he gets there—when he's about halfway—you're going to "change your mind" and call him back to you instead. Call loud enough for him to hear you, and happily as always when outdoors.

Most dogs will naturally have no initial interest coming when called. But since you're holding the leash, you can use it to stop him, calling him away from the plate and back to you. Then, when your dog is near, one at a time, give him *several* of the higher value treats and shower your dog with praise. This is called a jackpot because your dog receives even more than he expected. He'll feel lucky and, most importantly, he'll remember how he won that jackpot. He did it by running back *to* you when what he initially wanted was to run *away* from you. And that is the recall we all need in an emergency!

After the jackpot, release him to the plate so he can go back and get that first one. Score again!

As time goes on, play the Paper Plate Recall in varied ways, sometimes letting him eat the treat on the plate, and sometimes calling him back mid-way. Once you notice that your dog understands, you can try it without the leash or transition to a lighter line before you eliminate it altogether. Although the plate served as a target, an obvious distraction, eventually you can try to eliminate it, dropping a few kibbles on the ground. Now he'll have a stronger distraction consisting of both the ground and the food.

Here are a few benefits of the game from your dog's perspective. First, he'll think, wow, my owner knows where all the good stuff is. I should listen to him when he calls. It could be important. Second, he will come to understand that sometimes you let him investigate what he wanted in the first place, but only after he checks in with you. Third, you are no longer a spoilsport. In fact, you're the opposite. You are the provider of good things.

Ping-Pong Recall

The Ping-Pong Recall game is useful when you want to include a friend or family members. This is an especially good activity to get your children involved in the care and education of the family pet. You can also make it a game for your children as well. Your dog becomes the ping-pong ball, running and bouncing back and forth in between you and a partner. You'll quickly be able to add more people to the mix.

All these recall games are designed to teach a similar lesson—that it is important to listen at all times, because I may need you for something better than what you're doing right now. The Ping-Pong Recall plays into this by making sure that your dog learns to listen to different family members and signals, and he must resist any impulse to run away chasing something.

Once again, we'll start the dog on a long line to better help him learn the structure of this activity. You can hold the line at first. Use a 15- to 20-foot leash. Make sure you have attached the line to a noncorrective collar because you may need to use the line to stop your dog from running in the wrong direction. Although you will want to

Your dog becomes the ball, flying from one family member to another when called.

stop him so you can redirect him to the right place, you don't want him to think he's in trouble.

Flat nylon collars with a buckle or snap are best for this game—and most games—where you might need to change where your dog is headed. In the beginning, you might want to wear gloves if you have a strong, fast dog. Imagine a 70-pound golden retriever running hard in the wrong direction, and you have to stop him with a nylon line or leash. Even garden gloves will help prevent friction burn. And if your dog is super excitable, you might even want to begin indoors. If your dog is very responsive and you're playing in a fenced area, you may dispense with the leash at your discretion.

Start with only two people to keep it simple, but if you wish, you'll be able to integrate more participants soon. Both people should have easily accessible treats, and, in this case, both should have the same kind of treat.

During this game, we will alternate roles with our partner. One person will be the "caller" and the other will be "neutral." Any time you are neutral, you should turn away from the dog, looking away with a straight face. You will appear to be uninterested in what is happening, hence, "neutral." The person acting as the caller should be excited, vibrant, making eye contact with the dog. Playing these roles as described will make it far easier for your dog to understand who he should come to at any given moment.

Start by standing about 6 feet away from each other. The person holding the leash will start as neutral, ignoring the dog. The other person starts by happily calling the dog, bending toward him in a gesture that resembles a play bow, clapping hands, asking the dog to come.

As the dog begins to run to the caller, the person holding the leash must ensure the dog has enough slack to get there. Adjust your leash grip as needed. As the dog runs to the caller, the neutral takes a few steps back, increasing the distance a little bit for the next call.

Once the dog comes to the caller, that person gives him a treat.

As the game gets going, you can hold the very end of the line to prevent your dog from running off if he gets distracted by a bird. If traffic is not a concern, if you're within a fenced area, you can let go of the line and let it drag behind as your dog gains confidence and skill. Eventually you won't need the leash at all.

Now it is the neutral person's turn to be the caller. The first caller turns away from the dog and becomes neutral. The new caller calls the dog and, as he is running, the neutral takes a few steps back. Once the dog gets to the caller, give him a treat.

Ping-pong your dog back and forth a few times, each time walking a bit further back and taking turns on who is neutral and who is the caller.

Once you have some good distance between the people and your dog understands this part of the game, it's a good time to break off until next time. A good rule of thumb for this game is to quit while you're ahead and your dog is still enjoying herself.

Next time you play, review by starting as you did before for just a couple of recalls. Then it's time to add a twist. One person will call the dog, clapping their hands while the other person goes neutral. But once the dog runs about halfway, the caller will go

The ping-pong recall offers good learning and exercise opportunities.

neutral and turn away while the neutral person switches the game by clapping and calling the dog back.

Suddenly, your dog needs to realize that the situation has changed. She has to learn to stop, switch direction, and run back toward the caller. If she continues to run to the (now) neutral person, the neutral person should not acknowledge the dog. Turn away, don't give her a treat, and completely ignore the dog. The "correct" person who was calling her should gently pick up the line, walking the dog back to where she should have come. Then quietly give her a treat in the location she was supposed to come back to. Thus, the dog learns that only the *active* caller offers the reward. Moreover, the active caller can change at any moment so he should remain aware rather than act by rote.

Play until he realizes he needs to come to the person who is actively calling him at the moment. Then call it a success and break off for a while. If you add additional people, form a large triangle or square. It's the same game you first taught him but with more players.

Eventually, your dog will learn to retain situational awareness of voices and body language. He'll learn that the destination he thought was going to provide him with the most reward can change at any time, and—critically—he is going to learn that the person actively calling him is the one who is going to reward him the most.

Once he understands, this game works best when you only do the "switch caller" routine about 25 percent of the time because you do not want him to expect the switch. You want him to listen for it, never knowing when it is coming, and otherwise assuming he should run all the way to the person calling him.

Ping-Pong Recall helps not only to exercise your dog in a productive way, but it also teaches him to *think* as he runs. And that is a great skill!

"I Changed My Mind" Recall

Our friend Mary has a border collie named Mia. She is a brilliant dog who easily learned all the most important behaviors. In what seemed like no time at all, Mary taught Mia to heel, sit, down, stay, and come. In the beginning she enjoyed each of her lessons. But she learned them almost too easily and quickly became bored. Mia became uninterested in obedience practice because she was a smart dog who wasn't being challenged. Eventually her willingness to follow commands began to suffer. She was also slightly difficult to live with, rarely settled, pacing, and constantly looking for something to do.

If you give hours' worth of multiplication tables to a talented high school student, one who is ready for the challenge of algebra, her attitude will suffer. That's how it went with Mary and Mia. At first training was a pleasure because Mia soaked up information eagerly like a sponge. But once the routines became too simplistic, Mia all but gave up. Like all good trainers, Mary wanted her dog's obedience training to be engaging so the dog would opt in rather than viewing the work as drudgery. But you can't force a dog to have fun. And you can't make them show interest when they don't want to. That why it is so effective to play games that appeal to your dog, and which you approach without pressure.

Mary deduced she needed to find games that were genuinely challenging to Mia, activities that would stimulate her mind. She wanted a game that had educational value and one that Mia would love. Complicating matters was that arthritis in Mary's knees restricted her own mobility. So, she needed a solution that would catch and hold Mia's attention but would not require Mary herself to run.

Mary's solution was to take advantage of Mia's obsession with toys and retrieving. Not only did Mia constantly want to play with her toys, but she would often drop one in Mary's lap or at her feet, almost demanding that her owner pick it up and throw it. Although Mary did this often, it was a game that Mia organized herself. And once Mary started to respond to these demands, she found her dog becoming more and more obsessive about it. That's when she realized she could make a bargain with the dog: I'll trade you a throw in return for some happy obedience practice.

She started by throwing a favored toy a far distance for Mia to retrieve. As in any game of fetch, Mia ran to the toy and happily brought it back. As a border collie, she did this with ease. Too much ease perhaps. Within a week, Mia would play the game but without the same sense of eagerness as at first. So, Mary changed it up again. She introduced a recall component similar to calling the dog back from the midway point during the Ping-Pong Recall. She threw the toy, released Mia from the sit to run get it, but then called her back when she was about halfway to the toy. The first time Mary did this, Mia stopped and turned toward her, slightly confused . . . because this was very different. Without sounding irritated, Mary repeated the *come* command in order to clarify for Mia who seemed to be asking, "Are you sure?" Mia came right back. Mary asked her to sit, praised her warmly and then sent her back out to retrieve the toy as a reward for the recall.

Mia loved the game . . . for a month.

Border collies were bred for their ability to handle complex work far away from their owners. Sheep can easily be grazing a half mile from where the owner is standing. The dog may need to bunch them up, then move them all the way back toward the owner, including stragglers. Not only can this breed eventually learn to cope with that level of complexity, they actually crave it. Moreover, they may exhibit anxious or even obsessive behaviors if they don't get it in some form. The same can also be true of other breeds and even mixed breed dogs. Highly motivated, intelligent dogs easily become bored with simplistic games. They require variables to maintain interest.

Though the "call back from halfway, sit, and then go back to get the toy" game was fun, even that became too easy for this intelligent dog.

To add variables to the game, Mary provided a series of more complex challenges. Most of the time, Mia was asked to go retrieve the toy. But, at any moment, she might be asked to perform a different task, such as one of these:

- Come back from about halfway.
- Come back from most of the way, mere inches from the retrieve object.
- Sit in front of the toy before grabbing it.
- Lie down before being released to retrieve the toy.
- Lie down halfway to the toy.
- Go get the toy, drop the toy halfway back, come back and sit, then go back and get the toy.

And on and on and on. The variables added an infinite variety of options so that every day the game was interesting. It was never the same two days in a row. Much like herding sheep.

For Mia, this new, more complex way of playing the game is thrilling. Although she is 9 years old now, she eagerly awaits the game nearly every day. She and Mary continue to play most days.

Opposite page: *You can introduce variables such as laying down near the toy before bringing it back.*

Of course, not every dog is like Mia. Some individual dogs or breeds don't like this much complexity. But most dogs do enjoy playing with a toy you have thrown. It is instinctual and appeals to their prey drive. You can create variables and complexity, depending on the breed and your dog's overall interest in playing. The best game is one your dog looks forward to.

So, to summarize, here is how to apply the "I Changed My Mind" Recall to your dog.

- Start with fetch, using a toy the dog likes. Initially use a 15- to 20-foot leash to help keep your dog coming to you with the toy.

- Toss the toy a short distance to start, reeling the dog in if necessary. Offer him a treat. If he drops the toy instead of bringing it to you, quietly pick it up. Briefly ignore your dog then try again.

- When your dog responds, offer a treat. Toss the ball again, gradually speeding up the routine. Treat after every retrieve.

- When he's doing this consistently, introduce the interruption. When he is halfway to the toy, use the leash to stop him and call him back happily. Be patient with this and stay upbeat and positive. It may take several attempts for him to start to get it.

- When he does come back, offer a second toy, a better one such as an interesting squeaky toy, for him to play with briefly. Then pocket it, go get and toss the original toy. You may need to lead him back to it initially to remind him of what you're asking.

- Send him all the way to the toy and have him bring it back 75 percent of the time. But then occasionally give him the opportunity to stop midway and come back to play with the second toy.

Once your dog masters this game, feel free to introduce new challenges and experiences as Mary did with Mia. Many dogs are perfectly content with just the halfway and come back part of the game, while others may enjoy more challenges to keep the game interesting.

Practicing Recall Games for the Fun and Safety of Your Dog

One of the best parts about these recall games is that dogs love them. They are active games that cause your dog to use his brain as well as his body. Therefore, the activity is both mentally and physically productive. You wind up with a dog who feels more fulfilled, more connected to you, and more obedient.

As dog trainers, we love games that teach valuable life safety skills. Recall games teach concepts that will help keep your dog safer, and also make it easier for you to enjoy activities with him. And you'll be able to call him back at any time.

CHAPTER 4

Fetch for Adolescent and Adult Dogs

Fetch is the most classic game ever played between human and dog, and it was probably the first game. But we will never know who invented it: People? Or dogs?

Dogs were domesticated tens of thousands of years ago. Research suggests they are the descendants of Asian and European wolves. The process was probably slow. The earliest animals who were to become dogs crept around the edges of human habitats, feeding on scraps. Perhaps the first wolf-dog puppies were safer when whelped in dens near the scent of humans, afforded a measure of protection from larger predators by the presence of people. No doubt they were eventually encouraged and even fed when they became worth their calories as the first early alert warning system against intruders of all species. Does your dog become alert at a foreign noise, even from outside? Does he bark through the window at passersby? This is instinctual behavior that dates back 30,000 years and is probably the first useful thing a live animal ever did for who *we* became, Homo sapiens.

We'll never know when the first man, woman, or child threw the first stick, but it's not beyond imagining that it took place thousands of years ago when domestication first began. Perhaps an early dog or puppy followed a villager who was busy with a chore. We can picture the dog picking up a stick and spontaneously prancing with it, eventually dropping it close by his amused companion. How natural it would have been for the villager to pick up the stick and toss it, noticing how eagerly the dog chased after it, happily bringing it back as if to say, 'Do it again!'. Who knows? But one thing is certain: over the centuries fetch has morphed into the most popular game humans play with their dogs, an activity that is deeply bonding and can even be an instrument of healing in the human/dog relationship.

We recall a friend of the monastery who brought his well-bred German shepherd female to us for training while Marc was visiting New Skete. Daisy was a nice-looking 2-year-old from a good kennel in Pennsylvania. She was friendly and had excellent temperament, but she constantly exhibited signs of anxiety. The most notable symptom was that any time Daisy wasn't eating or sleeping, she whined, paced, and could not settle or relax. When outdoors in a field, unlike the other dogs in our care, Daisy would not run, play, explore or use her nose to connect to the environment. Daisy had anxiety and she was confused.

As trainers, we have met others like her over the years. Most dogs thrive on work, doing some sort of job, even if it is as simple as fetching a stick or keeping a watchful eye over their property. Normally anxious dogs respond very well to the structured routine in our training program. A predictable schedule consisting of work, rest and play soothes an anxious dog's nerves, erasing any vague or unreasonable fear of the unknown. We wrote extensively about how to create a healthy routine in *Let Dogs Be Dogs*, and that's what we did for Daisy. But it wasn't quite working until we added a play component.

She ate breakfast and dinner at the same time every day. She was let out to potty on a regular schedule that she quickly came to understand. Each day at the same hour, Daisy went on the sort of Purposeful Walk we detail in *The Art of Training Your Dog*. Here at New Skete, the monks each handle a dog so we can lead a small group at once. We hike a long gravel road that slopes downhill through our woods. We often see squirrels, chipmunks, rabbits, and even the occasional deer. This purposeful walk, with each dog calmly walking next to a trainer, teaches them to remain focused on their human, respectful of their most important job requirement: keep the leash loose. In other words, pulling is off the table. That being said, although we teach the dogs to remain calm, they love the sights, sounds and smells of nature and they get to experience all of that on the walk. After the walk, we come back to the training center and work on sit and down stays, come when called, and other obedience exercises. Then it's back to the kennel, where the dogs generally take a well-deserved nap.

Ninety-nine percent of dogs respond so well to this routine that those with anxiety quickly feel and behave better. Those who are simply unruly learn to respond to commands and be more polite. But none of that worked very well for Daisy. Yes, she went on all the walks. Yes, she did all the training sessions. But she did all of them while quivering, tense, and nearly unable to keep the leash loose despite instruction. She complied, but barely. Our sense was that she wasn't belligerently refusing to behave. She just couldn't. In the kennel, rather than nap like the other dogs during rest time, Daisy paced and whined. What we do every day to help dogs just wasn't working for Daisy, and that concerned us. She was friendly. She wanted to be close to people. But she wanted something that even she couldn't understand. It was as though Daisy had way too much energy and drive bottled up inside with no way to release it.

We realized that we were going to have to add something to the mix. Once we build a reliable recall—the *come* command—we sometimes begin to throw a ball for a dog to chase down and bring back. Many dogs enjoy running after the ball, but we usually have to teach them to bring it right back and give it to us. Left to their own devices, many dogs will play "keep away" rather than fetch. Although they may enjoy that, it certainly doesn't lead to better behavior.

We took Daisy to the field on a long leash and tossed the ball in front of her. She watched it plop on the ground, never moving from our side, trembling nervously as always. Marc picked it up, showed it to her, and threw it again, farther this time. Daisy was completely uninterested. Brother Christopher had to get the ball to bring it back, and she seemed to wonder why we were throwing and retrieving a ball in the first place. Silly trainers, she must have thought. This is unusual, as the average German shepherd loves to chase a ball. We took her back to the kennel, slightly defeated but pondering.

Sometimes a dog will not respond to a certain kind of toy. Others just have limited interest in any toy. But we had to find a way to get Daisy engaged with running and playing to drain her of the energy that was bottled up inside her. We were convinced the roots of her anxiety were planted in energy and intelligence, with no way to express them. Therefore, we theorized, she was under great pressure with no way to release it other than anxiety behaviors such as whining, pacing, and trembling.

Although most dogs like a tennis ball, Daisy did not. Over the next few days,

Some dogs have no response to a certain toy, like a ball, yet may love another.

we tried playing with her with a wide variety of objects that ranged from retrieving bumpers to rope toys and even squeaky toys. Nothing. She watched us closely, far more interested in our antics than anything we were taking turns tossing in an attempt to encourage her to react. Until we were down to one last hope. We dug out a foam throwing disc one of us had been given at a dog trainers' conference. We took Daisy to the field, wiggled it front of her face. She looked at it. Then Brother Christopher sailed it 8 feet in front of her. Though she didn't run to it, she did watch where it landed. Rather than pressure her to move toward it, possibly ruining her interest, we praised her lavishly just for looking. Marc picked up the disc, tucked it under his arm and moved her around the field a bit. Then he repeated the toss.

This time Daisy ran a step or two toward it before abandoning the idea and running back to Brother Christopher. We praised her more quietly this time. Again, Marc tucked the disc under his arm and moved around the field, and before we stopped walking, he made a surprise throw. Daisy ran to that purple foam disc and stood over it. We held our collective breath. She looked at us, but we looked away so as not to distract her with our stares. When we looked back, she was nosing at the disc, and finally *she picked it up*!

It was the beginning of an amazing turnaround for this dog. In short order she discovered the retrieve drive that had been lurking untapped inside her. We spent days hurling and retrieving the disc. Incredibly, once that genie was out of the bottle, when Daisy saw a ball on the ground, she brought it to Marc, wagging as though she was quite pleased to show him that she finally understood. Within another few days, we were using a ball launcher to throw the ball 50 yards, giving Daisy a mental and physical workout she had never had before. We began to mix obedience commands, such as sit or down, between the throws and she did those with joy, understanding that they were the key to being released to the ball.

Within 2 weeks the anxiety melted away and Daisy no longer trembled, paced, or whined as before. Instead, when she wasn't working or playing, Daisy did something she had never done before. She napped. To this day, several years after training, her owner reports that Daisy loves to chase and retrieve any toy thrown for her. They play daily and Daisy is happy, well-adjusted, and not nervous.

A true game of fetch is fun but also teaches cooperation.

The status of fetch as one of the best games for dogs is well deserved. That's why it plays such a large role in this book. Fetch is the single most engaging game you can play with a dog of almost any age. Although it varies a little when dealing with young puppies, which we have covered in Chapter 9 (page 155), the average dog will happily play a game of fetch well into advanced age.

We have never met a dog who could not learn and profit from this game because—at its best—retrieving provides a great combination of exercise peppered with moments of self-control. Of course, dogs and humans don't always see fetch the same way. A productive game of fetch is one where you and your dog are in sync and know what to expect from one another. An unproductive game of fetch is undisciplined, uncontrolled . . . and extremely common. First, let's define the term "fetch," or, as we sometimes call it, "retrieve." We'll use both terms interchangeably throughout the chapter. But before we define it for you, let's give you your *dog's* definition of the game, because that is probably what you have been playing.

Here's how the game works in your dog's mind:

I bark and nudge. Maybe I drop a toy in your lap. Then you throw it. I run and grab it. I run around with the toy. You call me back. But why would I give you my new favorite toy so quickly? Ha! Not going to do that. It's mine. I like it. I'm keeping it. Buddy, what you call fetch, I call "keep away," and it's a much better game because you run and chase me.

You may think you're playing fetch. But your dog is playing a completely different game, one which he invented and which he loves. Still, although your dog may find this activity great fun, it doesn't teach the concepts that we're after for the purposes of this book—purposeful play and better behavior.

In fact, when a game of fetch devolves into keep away, it actually rewards your dog more for disobedience than it does for collaboration. *Not* listening to you becomes more rewarding than going along with your commands and requests. When playing keep away, your dog learns that "crime pays." It may seem harmless enough and although it is better to play with your dog than to not play, accidentally rewarding uncooperative behavior can have negative consequences in other areas of your relationship.

For example, in real life, when your dog picks up a forbidden object, like a chicken

Playing "keep away" is not as productive as playing fetch.

bone that has fallen on the kitchen floor, you urgently ask for it back. But your dog remembers all the times he ran away with his desired object and you chased him. That sounds like much more fun. Plus, he knows he might be able to gulp the bone while you're running after him, swearing. This game could end with a trip to the vet—or worse.

A dog trainer's definition of fetch is different from a dog's.

Although it's still a game your dog will enjoy, it must be taught in stages. Like all the games we teach in this book, your dog is going to learn to play *your way* so he can get the joy *he* wants while you get the benefits that *you* want.

Playing Fetch the Dog Trainer's Way

Most dogs have some degree of prey drive. Prey drive is the instinct that motivates wolves to chase and catch. Without it, they would not be able to thrive. For tens of thousands of years, wolves were a highly successful species on multiple continents. That held true until humans became their competition and severely reduced their population. Our dogs are no longer wolves, just as elephants are no longer mastodons, but they are still predators, and the DNA trail is unmistakable. From the teacup chihuahua who grabs the squeaky toy and shakes it, all the way through the Great Dane who runs a 50-yard dash to catch a tennis ball, the instinct driving your dog at those moments is prey drive, her desire to chase after movement. The chihuahua shakes the squeaky toy because it emulates how he would quickly dispatch a rodent. And the Great Dane runs down the ball because he doesn't have a boar to chase, as his ancestors were bred to do.

Of course, we feed our modern dogs very well. They no longer have to sing for their supper as they did in the wild and through most of their history with humankind. But instinct is genetic, hard wired, and powerful. We deny or attempt to suppress it at our own risk. That's because these vestigial instincts and desires are so deeply engrained in the dog sleeping next to you that he will find a way to express them if you do not help him use them productively. Keep away, mouthing the cat and shredding the couch are not good ways for him to use his mouth. Yet these are the ways his instincts will leak out of him if you don't organize them into something useful.

You will find mentions of fetch sprinkled throughout a variety of the games in this book. But this chapter will help you with the foundational concepts that make them all work for more purposeful play and better behavior. We want to help our dogs realize that *we* are the reward, that *we* control the play (and the prey), that we know when the toy or ball will launch, and the game continues as long as he follows the rules.

Conversely, if we merely respond to the dog's demands to throw the ball and let him play with no guidance, we quickly become irrelevant. The dog will view us as human tennis ball launchers with no meaningful opinions. The social contract below, between you and your dog, is what makes this the most important game you can play with your dog. Here are the promises both you and your dog should make:

- I will throw the ball for you.
- I will make the game interesting.
- But I want you to start with a moment of control (a sit, or quietly wait).
- When I have thrown the object, you get it joyfully.
- You bring it back directly.
- Then drop it or hand it to me.

- I will ask you to follow another quick command (*sit* or *down*) for an organized moment of cooperation.

- Then I will release you and throw it again.

By weaving control into the game of retrieve, we wind up with a tapestry of well-organized and useful behavior instead of an unrecognizable jumble of yarn.

Although we have asserted that all dogs have some level of prey drive, we also understand that there are breed differences, and the level of both interest and ability in fetch can vary wildly from breed to breed and between individuals.

Dogs who are interested in chasing virtually any toy that you may throw are the easiest to teach. That's because you don't have to awaken a hidden interest in chasing an object: you merely need to teach them to bring it back and allow you to take it. We will discuss details of achieving that later in this chapter.

But first, let's talk about a dog who does not exhibit a high level of interest in a toy you throw. While it is true that not every game will suit every dog, and that you should pick those that appeal to your dog, understand many dogs who start with little to no interest in fetch can indeed learn this game. In fact, some of these converts

Dogs learn to bring the toy back directly, then drop or give in return for the next throw.

become the most enthusiastic retrievers of all. The trick is to start slow, with very low pressure, and most critically of all to find a toy that they actually like. You would be surprised how difficult that can be. And that causes some owners to give up too early.

Marc and his partner own a female rat terrier named Scooter. As a terrier, her favorite activity has always been sniffing outdoors and exploring Marc's property that he calls the Little Dog Farm. Over the years, Marc tried many times to throw various types of balls or toys to awaken what should have been Scooter's natural prey drive, but she never responded. In fact, unlike the purpose of her breed, which is to kill vermin, Scooter only got part of the genetic prey drive. She liked to sniff them out, then show them to Marc's Australian shepherd mix, Tippy, for the final dispatch.

Not getting a reaction meant Marc couldn't awaken prey drive on which to build a game of fetch. Nothing worked, so he gave up on the idea. However, when Scooter was about 10 years old, Marc found a small plush toy about 4 inches long in the shape of a dachshund. It was red, soft, and contained a squeaker. With very low expectations, Marc squeaked and threw the toy.

Although Scooter had ignored a decade's worth of squeaky toys, this one appealed to her for reasons unknown. She instantly pounced on it, shook and played with it, then dropped it in Marc's hand when he called her to come. Ten years old, and she finally found a toy she loved with all her little terrier heart. She was still interested in it, so Marc threw it and she pounced again. Thus ensued the first game of fetch she had ever played. They enjoyed 15 minutes of nonstop play. Out of the blue, Scooter had discovered her soulmate toy. At 17 years old now, she is too blind to fetch a toy, but she still enjoys using her nose, exploring the Little Dog Farm.

The moral of the story is that even if your dog is not interested in chasing or retrieving, it's possible you just haven't found your dog's soulmate toy. Don't be afraid to experiment. Slowly work your way through the variety of toys you probably own including balls, squeaky toys, rope toys, plush toys and throwing discs. Try two of them per day. If you throw the kitchen sink at your dog all at once, inevitably a bit of frustration will creep into your voice and you'll put your dog off the experience. So, we want to approach this with no pressure, like a low-key social experiment.

If you're watching TV or any other activity that doesn't especially distract your dog, casually throw a new toy and see if he has interest. Try a few times with the same toy If he has no reaction, wait a few minutes then try again with a different one. If you go through all your toys over time, it's probable that, like Scooter, your dog will discover the toy she didn't know she was waiting for her whole life. That will start a love affair that you can use to shape the concepts of retrieve which follow.

Martin Deeley, writer, retriever trainer, and top field competitor in the United Kingdom and the United States, was a friend of the authors who wrote books about teaching retrieve to hunting dogs. When Martin had difficulty with a dog who didn't want to retrieve, he told us that when all else failed, he would stuff a toy in a recently used white sock, tie a knot, and start the dog on that. More often than not, a sock would get the dog started. "They like things that smell like you," Martin told us, "So if you have to, begin with that and then later you can rub that sock on a new object or even put it inside the sock for a few throws. Many times, they will retrieve the new item because you have transferred the scent." Martin was a master at patiently motivating a dog to retrieve, and that is a secret worth learning.

It is also important for dog owners to understand that reluctance to retrieve can stem from having been repeatedly reprimanded for picking up objects around the house. After a while, sensitive dogs may begin to think they'll get in trouble for using their mouths that way. This is one reason why, in Chapter 9 (page 155) where we talk about puppies, we talk about gently removing forbidden objects from a puppy's mouth rather than dramatically pulling them away. Many of us have also adopted older dogs where we may not know their prior life experience, so we may need to do a little work do to help undo unwanted lessons they learned in the past.

Believe us when we tell you all this is worthwhile. Once a dog learns to retrieve, you will gain efficient exercise opportunities. Depending on your dwelling and the weather, you can exhaust even a big dog in 15 minutes. If the weather is inclement or you don't have much land for throwing, you can play in a basement or use long corridors in apartment buildings. After all, a tired dog is a good dog, and a good dog doesn't keep the neighbors awake with excessive barking. Because retrieve appeals so directly to your dog's genetic makeup, it is a deeply satisfying activity.

Some dogs will happily retrieve anything, but others are picky and prefer one toy over another.

Remember the story of Daisy?

She was the German shepherd who started with no visible retrieve drive, which meant that we could barely exercise her. This caused her to build up a great deal of anxiety and emotional suffering. But a patient approach to retrieve finally worked. For those dogs from whom you cannot find a preferred object despite your best efforts, we have one last trick up our sleeve to share with you. We suggest you try using food in the following way:

Place a handful of food in the middle of a dish towel and tie it up. This will create a very tempting object, but one that cannot easily be swallowed accidentally. Nonetheless, use it with supervision only. Depending on the dog, you may be able to put a handful of training treats in that object, but if you have a picky dog you may need to fill it with chunks of chicken breast or even cut up hot dogs.

Put your dog on a 15-foot leash to begin so that if he does pick up the towel, he can't run away with it and rip it apart. You have just turned that meaningless object into a potential gourmet meal, after all. We simply want your dog to learn that he should go get the package and bring it back to you so you can open it and give him a treat.

Let him quickly smell the towel and then, before he has a chance to snatch it from your hand, toss it forward a few feet. If he goes to it and sniffs, calmly praise. Don't pressure him or push him to do anything more. Wait quietly to see what he does. If he sniffs it and walks away, open it up and give him a treat. If he picks it up and brings it to you, even better. Give him a treat immediately from your pocket, but then also show him that if you open the towel, there is a better treat inside and give it to him.

Remember to use high-value food in the dish towel, something better than dry dog biscuits. Even dogs who don't show initial interest in retrieve usually pick up on this game: my owner throws something that smells like chicken; I go get it for her and she will give me some of what's inside. This works especially well if you practice before meals when your dog is hungry.

Once you've played this a few times, you have successfully achieved a game of fetch. You can then start to transition away from the towel. Eventually, whatever that treat was that you put inside will become a scent that he will understand. You can use it in other places. For example, you can take a plush toy, rub a hot dog on it, and then you can use that instead. Your dog should pick up on this quickly, and you'll be able to play fetch without having to sacrifice the entire linen closet.

- -

A Word of Warning: Expect the Unexpected

Be careful with this plan. The calmest dogs who are the least interested in this game may become enamored when you change the equation as we have described. We remember a black miniature poodle named Pippin who was owned by Mrs. and Dr. Anderson. The good doctor was a veterinarian, and his wife was training their dog to compete in the AKC Open Class, which requires retrieving.

But Pippin wanted nothing to do with any toy, let alone the regulation dumbbell used in competition. So, we decided to invent a reason for her to care about retrieving, and thus we dreamt up the "food in the object" routine. Because Pippin was relatively small, we used a white knee sock rather than a hand towel. The story has a happy ending, but Pippin sure taught us to use a hand towel instead of a sock.

We told Mrs. Anderson our idea so she could get started with the ill-fated sock at home. We asked her to bring a treat sock the following week. She appeared at the lesson and said, "Watch this."

She threw the tied-off sock 10 feet away. Pippin excitedly ran to it, picked it up, and brought it right to Mrs. Anderson, who opened it and fished out a tidbit of some kind. Thoroughly impressed, we asked if she was using hot dogs as we suggested. She cocked an eyebrow and said, "I am a gourmet chef. I do not have hot dogs in my kitchen. This is Duck a la Orange, lightly sauced."

Every week, Pippin got better and better at her retrieve. The training was successful, and we were ready to transfer her to a new object. But then, the unexpected happened.

Mrs. Anderson came in with the sock as usual, threw it, and sent the dog to retrieve it. Pippin only got halfway back before this overly smart little poodle thought of a way to get her treat faster. She tried to swallow the entire stuffed white sock, like a snake unhinging its jaw.

We ran to her in a panic but by then a bit of sock was down her throat. All we could think of was, what will Dr. Anderson say if he has to remove a large knee sock from the intestinal tract of his own dog?!

We managed to extract the knee sock with great effort because Pippin didn't want to spit it out. Once we had it in our possession, we looked at Mrs. Anderson and asked, "What the heck is in this thing?"

With a sigh of relief, she gave us her Andouille sausage recipe. We opened the sock, gave Pippin a piece, and put an order in for 2 pounds of sausage. Then we quickly transferred the dog to another object, making a mental note to thereafter use only larger objects that cannot be swallowed. Let this be a lesson. Be careful what you wish for because you might just get it. If you take the time to teach a happy retrieve with no pressure, even if you have to get creative, don't be surprised if your dog loves the game even more than you do.

Once you have transitioned to a new object, you can experiment with objects that you can throw further. Often, getting the hang of the first object will awaken hidden drive that even the dog didn't realize she had. That's what happened with Daisy. If you have space, even people who do not throw well can launch a ball using a handheld plastic ball launcher available at most pet stores, and that means that your throwing range can easily go to a hundred or more feet.

Daisy had anxiety caused by inadequate exercise. The constant tension in her brain meant that she never learned how to relax. She had no off switch. Ten throws of a tennis ball at a hundred feet each meant that a previously nervous dog would come inside and sleep for hours. Best of all, it only took about 15 minutes.

Teaching Retrieve the Easy Way

It is deceptively simple to frame the game of fetch the way that we, as dog trainers, suggest.

Attach a 15- or 20-foot leash to your dog's flat collar. Don't use a training collar when playing with a long lead so the dog won't get stopped short accidentally. Show the toy to your dog but don't tease him with it. You just want him to know you have it. Start with a moment of control by asking him to sit. Quickly release him from the sit with an *OK, go get it!* as you throw the toy only a few feet ahead of you. Throwing short prevents your dog from hitting the end of the leash and also keeps the initial excitement down to a manageable level.

When your dog picks up the toy, his first instinct may be to play with it or to pick it up and run away. Rather than issuing commands, simply turn and walk away with your back to the dog. Don't jerk the line but get him moving toward you, and as you walk away, reel in the leash, bringing him closer. Once he is close, turn around, kneel, and hold out a treat. Encourage your dog to come to you. If he doesn't drop the toy, tell him *give*, and place the treat right on his nose. Smoothly take the toy and hide it from sight as he eats the treat. Within a few tries, your dog should be coming directly to you from a short distance and offering up the toy for a treat. Over time, we will increase the distance thrown and reduce the treats to occasional, as an unexpected bonus.

Pro Tip: Never be in a rush to grab the toy away from your dog.

Martin Deeley told us that another of his secrets was to pet the dog before taking the toy. Allow him to hold it and use the leash gently to prevent him from running away. Then pet him on his body, not on his head. Slowly pet your way to his head, smoothly changing from petting to placing your hands on the toy. Chances are he'll release it now when you ask. Once you have the toy, ask your dog to sit, and then repeat. We believe that the reason dogs tend to guard toys is because of our own human tendency to try to grab them too quickly. This awakens the dog's instinct to guard and possess it. Martin found a way around that cycle, and it usually works.

Once your dog gets used to coming back with the toy, you can begin throwing a bit

Start with a sit. Your first toss should be short for better control.

Throw shorter than the length of the line so the dog will not be abruptly stopped short by the leash.

As your dog gets close, encourage her back to you.

farther and even drop the line, but we urge you to leave the line on the dog until you build reliability. That's because if he ever decides he's going to run past you to play his old favorite game of "keep away," you can simply step on the line and reel him in, organically stopping that game without scolding him.

Reprimands and pressure are not your friends when playing retrieve. Focused control, alternated with excitement, are the benefits of retrieve.

Once you have mastered this skill with your dog, you can add variations to the game.

For example, you can practice leash walking with your dog's favorite toy tucked under your chin where he can see it, and this will encourage him to heel while focusing on you rather than on distractions around you. You can also hide a toy in your pocket and practice obedience exercises such as recall with your dog, even playing some of the recall games in Chapter 3 (page 43), but then take a quick break to produce the surprise toy and throw it to add an exciting element as a reward.

ALWAYS LEAVE YOUR DOG WANTING MORE

Some dogs will happily retrieve until they nearly fall over from exhaustion. Others peter out and begin to lose interest after only a few throws. Gauge your dog's interest level and quit the game while your dog is hoping for at least one more throw. This builds drive so he's even more enthusiastic the next time you play. However, if you wait until your dog quits on you, you may actually reduce his drive. Always leave him wanting just a little more. You can always build his drive and stamina slowly over time.

FETCH IS A CLASSIC

There is a reason that fetch is the most classic game you can play with your dog. All her instincts crave it because it is based on the prey drive long baked into her DNA. It is stimulating not only for her body, but, critically, also for her mind. It burns off some of the extra energy and anxiety that many dogs accumulate from sitting at

home all day. And perhaps most important of all, you control the game. That makes you very, very important to your dog. *You* become the most valuable resource, someone not only to be loved but also respected.

We'll never know for sure. But it's entirely possible the first dog ever given a name was named because he wanted to play fetch.

CHAPTER 5

Games for a Rainy Day

*How to Drain Your Dog's Energy
When You Can't Go Outside*

Both the Monks of New Skete and Marc live in challenging weather regions, upstate New York and Chicago. We experience days or weeks when pouring rain or freezing conditions may make it nearly impossible to safely spend more than a few minutes outside. Such extremes are not uncommon. Arizona weather can reach as high as 120 degrees, enough to limit productive exercise to only a few minutes at a time. In Minnesota, subzero temperatures can hurt small dogs in 10 minutes or less.

On these "rainy days," Marc works with client dogs in his indoor training center then keeps himself occupied by conducting video chat consultations with dog owners, writing, and catching up on the news. Brother Christopher also trains indoors with clients on such days. He and the other monks conduct twice daily religious services and keep themselves busy with choir practice, study, meetings, and chores. When unable to spend significant time outside, both the Monks and Marc have plenty of work and leisure activity to prevent boredom.

But dogs only have the activities we actively provide for them. They get bored the same way people do. When a person is bored, we turn on a movie, work out, cook a meal, or call a friend. We find ways to occupy our minds and bodies to feel purposeful and content.

When an unattended dog gets bored, he is forced to invent his own entertainment. He will turn to a doglike activity that is natural for his species. The problem is, the game he assigns himself will likely involve chewing the furniture, chasing the cat, or barking hysterically at anything on the other side of a window. Dogs are intelligent, social beings. They're also domesticated predators, and—left to their own devices—their idea of fun is likely to be very different than yours.

That's why, on days where it's not safe or possible to take your dog outside for long walks or adventures, you still need to find a way to engage your dog's mind and body. He needs the stimulation, and you need a way to prevent destructive boredom behaviors. You can do this by playing indoor rainy-day games with your dog.

Not Just for Bad Weather Days

Rainy-day games are, of course, great for inclement days. But they'll also come in handy at other times and for other reasons. Certain dogs and owners may have mobility issues that make extended periods of time outdoors difficult. The activities we will present in this chapter offer ways to keep your dog occupied when weather, mobility, or circumstance make staying outside difficult.

Tired Brain—Tired Dog

Like people, dogs have both physical and mental energy. Think of these as springs, winding tighter and tighter as the day goes on, waiting for a chance to release. Outdoors, a dog can work off both forms of drive through running, then stopping to inhale and analyze the myriad scents he will encounter. But indoors, it is not possible to burn off all that excess energy through physical activities. There is not enough space or stimulation.

Luckily, you can burn off energy in other ways. Think about when you must learn a new computer program or video game or even when you change from one brand of cell phone to another. We expend significant mental energy concentrating on the learning experience, solving the complex puzzles before us. "Cognitive fatigue" refers to that feeling of mental burnout you may feel after prolonged periods of focus and concentration. To recover, the mind requires a period of rest during which we switch to a simpler activity such as watching TV, or even taking a nap.

Dogs are the same. When the weather does not cooperate or mobility issues prevent you from taking your dog out for exercise, you can still tire out your pet by exercising his brain. These games push your dog to think and explore and use a lot of your dog's psychological energy so that he feels a release of both mental and physical drive.

Remember:

- Ideally, these activities will be engaging and fun for your dog. He might prefer one over the others just as you may prefer a specific board game or video game. Don't reprimand your dog if he doesn't immediately understand what he is supposed to do. Most dogs can learn to play these games with the proper training, but even if your dog never seems to pick it up, as long as he has fun and is trying to figure out what you want, then the game did its job.

- Indoor games take time to learn. Your dog will learn how to play them in days or weeks, not minutes or hours. Start with easy steps and make them progressively more challenging only when your dog has mastered each step and starts to get bored.

- Because learning takes time, there is no harm if you start training early—even without a rainy day. The earlier your dog learns these activities, the more fun they'll be on days when weather or mobility prevents you from going outside.

FIND IT

A dog's sense of smell is thousands of times keener than our own, with the scent center occupying a huge part of a dog's brain. When we smell a rose, for example, our brains say, "This smells like a rose," and then, over time—even if we are still near the flower—we slowly stop noticing the scent.

When a dog smells a rose, his brain says, in essence, "This is a Damask rose, and there is still a drop of dew on this rose from last night. The rose bloomed last week. Also, 4 hours ago, another dog sniffed this rose. That dog was female."

A dog's nose picks up individual scents and smells that are far more nuanced than anything we can imagine. They also never get used to the smell. Their brains continue to pick up and always analyze scent molecules. Surely you have noticed your dog not only sniff an object or the air but continue to do so for such a prolonged time that it looks like he has entered a trance. That's because his olfactory system picks up scent molecules and actually *concentrates* them. For the dog, the smell does not fade over time as for us. Rather, it gathers strength.

We can use that ability to create fun, indoor activities that will excite and tire out a dog. The act of sniffing—if it is given structure and purpose—will use a lot of brain power and leave your dog feeling satisfied with the experience.

The Find It game teaches your dog to use his sense of smell to find an object you will hide in progressively more difficult places. Use a toy that your dog especially likes, better yet if it's a toy that allows you to stuff a treat inside. Or you can take a tennis ball, cut a slit, squeeze the ball, and place a treat inside. Use a treat that has a strong, delicious smell such as a raisin-sized chunk of hot dog, something that your dog will work hard to earn. It's better to start when your dog is hungry rather than shortly after a meal.

- First, have your dog sit/stay. If you haven't yet learned how to train your dog to sit and stay correctly, we teach techniques for this in our book *The Art of Training Your Dog*. If your dog still has a bit of a hard time with sit/stay when a treat is involved, you can have someone else hold your pet on a leash or tie the leash somewhere that is safe for your dog.

- First let your dog sniff the object. Be gentle about it but don't give it to him. Rub the toy along the floor stopping somewhere across the room but within his line of sight. In a pleasant tone, say *find it*, and let him go after the toy. Since it is in his line of sight, he should get to it very fast, but he will notice the smell along the ground and naturally find himself following it.

- When he gets to the toy, he'll want to mouth and play with it. *Do not grab it away from him*. Instead, pet him all over his body while he has it in his mouth. If he moves away from you, put a leash on your dog next time so you don't have to chase or grab him. You can simply hold the leash while you pet him.

- Pet your way toward his head and then gently remove the toy from his mouth. Fish the treat out of the toy and give it to your dog but you keep the toy itself.

- To build the dog's desire for the toy, reserve it for this game only.

Chasing your dog around the house to take the toy or removing it from your dog using negative tones is a bit like coaching a Little League baseball team of third graders and yelling at them. Be gentle and motivational without becoming irritated if he doesn't immediately understand, or over excited if he does. If your dog is likely to try to take the toy and run away from you, attach a light leash so that you can gently redirect him back to you without making a big deal about it. Keep things very light and positive.

Repeat three to five times per session. Play one to three sessions per day spread throughout the day. It's tempting to keep playing, but dogs can get tired of games that are too easy or played too often, and we want him to be excited to play again, every time.

After one or two sessions, start making the game more difficult. After all, we haven't used much nose yet.

- Drag the toy along the floor as before, but this time you'll place it just out of sight. Your dog will observe you, so we know it won't take too much nose at this stage. However, we're slowly building toward blind hides that will require understanding and a persistent nose. Hide the object just around a corner or behind a table leg or curtain where your dog will only have to make a little more effort to find it. The toy should be easy to get to, but difficult to see from his starting point.

- Next, you'll want to stop rubbing the treat on the ground, forcing the dog to find the toy by smelling the air.

- Finally, you will want to start placing the toy in different parts of your home, perhaps introducing new toys (scented by the same familiar treat) and mixing it up so that your dog continues to enjoy the game and use the scent center of his brain.

Only add complexity once your dog has consistently mastered finding the toy. If your dog has difficulty with a new step, go back and try the previous step and try a simpler complexity until he has mastered it. We do want him to keep finding the toy and receiving the treat. A motivated dog who truly understands the game will happily look for the object until he finds it, even if it takes 10 or 15 minutes. It's also OK to give your dog hints now and then. It's all for fun.

We remember a time when Marc's Doberman, Diablo was in the veterinary hospital for nearly a week. Diablo's companion dog was named Angel, a female Doberman. Angel was distraught with Diablo's absence. She barely ate or slept, whining nonstop for 3 solid days.

On a Tuesday morning Marc visited Diablo in the hospital. A vet tech walked the dog through a door into the waiting room where Marc sat in one row of chairs. After the visit, the tech took Diablo back the same way they had come.

That night Marc took Angel with him to the vet's office to drop off one of his t-shirts for Diablo to sleep with. Scent is important to dogs and Marc knew this would comfort his dog. He and Angel walked into the vet office whereupon Angel, who had never been taught to track scent, put her nose to the ground, pulled Marc to the exact chair he had sat in that morning, lingered a moment and then—nose to the ground—pulled him to the door leading into the back where Diablo went. Marc left the shirt with the vet and took Angel home. She slept for 12 hours and ate a hearty meal. The nose knows.

THE TREADMILL TROT

When you can't go outside to exercise, bring the exercise indoors!

Treadmills have long been a way for humans to stay fit indoors, regardless of weather. They are among the most used machines at fitness centers across the country. Many people use treadmills and related technology, like stationary bikes, to keep themselves moving.

Treadmills can also be used for dogs. Ideally, you purchase a doggy treadmill that is made specifically for canines. They tend to be quieter and have side walls to make the space feel safer and prevent jumping off. Training tends to be easier too. But a

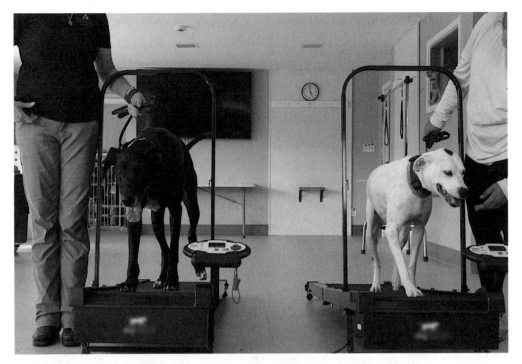

Treadmills offer a fun release of energy but you must follow safety protocols.

human treadmill will do if you introduce it carefully, make it a fun activity and most important of all, *observe safety rules we will discuss.* You can often find very economical used examples at secondhand stores or garage sales

Treadmills are a supervised activity. You must always stay with and observe your dog when using the treadmill. *Never tie a dog to the treadmill.* Never leave a dog alone on a treadmill. Violating these rules could cause serious injury.

Teaching your pet to use his machine is a slow and steady process. Take your time, because at first, a dog may worry about various aspects of a treadmill. It makes noise. It is large and odd-looking. It will eventually move under his feet. Be patient. The benefits of using it are worthwhile and when introduced the way we will describe, most dogs will come to look forward to trotting on the treadmill.

First, let's get used to the treadmill *without turning it on.* Here are the steps to introduce one at a time. Each step should take 3 days. But don't move to the next step until your dog is comfortable with the current stage. Some dogs may need more than

3 days per step. Please ignore the hundreds of videos online that show how to teach an unfamiliar dog to run on the treadmill within minutes. Our way is much safer and will lead to fun rather than stress. Safety first!

- Lead him to the treadmill (which is in the "off" position) with a treat placed at his nose. Encourage him to hop on or at least place one foot on the platform, then allow him to eat the treat.

- Occasionally place a treat onto the middle of the treadmill belt while still in the off position. He will find it and will begin to seek it of his own volition.

- You can begin to feed meals on the platform, placing the bowl where you'll eventually want his head. Help him place all four feet on the belt so he can eat while fully on the treadmill while it is still in the "off" position.

- Next, we'll get your dog used to the sound, so he won't be frightened. Place him on a leash. Stand well back from the machine but turn it on. Reward your dog with praise or treats until, over time, he will comfortably stand right next to the humming treadmill and take his treats or eat his meals.

You'll help your dog become accustomed to the treadmill's size, sound, and feel while also making him feel rewarded by it, all before he has ever been on it while it is moving. Stay positive and calm, no matter how he reacts. Pressuring the dog will be counterproductive. Patience is your best friend, so let your dog set the pace of how quickly you move through the steps. He may get stuck on one for a long time, or you may need to go back a step for a while. All of this is normal but worthwhile.

Once he is completely comfortable being on the turned off machine, and or near

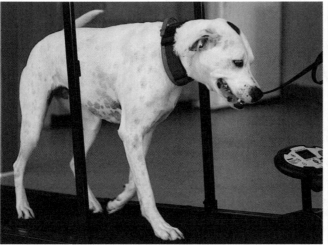
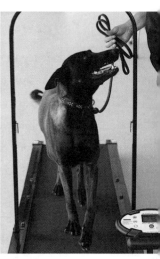

Never tie your dog to the machine. Keep the leash free of the moving belt.

the running treadmill, it's time to actually use it. Lead your leashed dog onto the belt while it still turned off. Hold the leash close to the dog so that he can't easily hop off and so that it can't get tangled in the moving belt. Turn on the treadmill to its slowest setting. Gently but quickly use the leash to prevent your dog from hopping off and speak calm encouraging words. As he begins to walk, remember to hold the leash so he doesn't hop off. Within a session or two, he'll be well used to the process and will look forward to it. If your dog seems frightened and doesn't quickly begin to walk on the slow-moving belt, turn off the machine. You can always go back a few steps and give it more time. A percentage of dogs may prefer some other activity instead, but most will learn this well if given time and patience.

Over several sessions, work your way up to trotting speed, never a full run. Unconditioned dogs will tire quickly. Start with only 2 minutes, but as your dog's stamina increases over time, you can slowly build up to 20 minutes. If your dog begins to tire, stop immediately. *Remember not to tie your dog to the treadmill or leave him unattended.* Trotting on the treadmill is both physically and mentally satisfying for your dog.

PUT AWAY YOUR TOYS

This is a game most easily taught to dogs who love to walk around with their toys. It makes for a great parlor trick to show guests and is a fun way to get a bit of help around the house.

For this, we'll need a command. We'll choose *put away*.

Call your dog to your side and place a big basket in front of him. If he's not immediately responsive, you can always use a leash. Give him a favorite toy and let him hold it for a few minutes.

Ultimately, we want to teach your dog to drop the toy in the basket. We're not teaching your dog that you're going to steal it, or that giving you the toy is the reward. So, we're not going to reach for it.

Instead, we're going to do the following:

- With the toy in his mouth, bring your leashed dog closer to the basket or bring the basket to your dog.

- Say *put away*, and holding a treat close to your dog's nose, quickly move it over the basket and drop the goodie in the bottom of the basket while the dog watches.

He is likely to drop the toy in the basket and go for the treat. If he does, praise warmly. If he drops the toy near the basket, but not inside, don't reprimand him. Allow him to take the treat and we'll help him better understand what we want without worrying or confusing him. After several repetitions, should he continue to drop the toy outside the basket, here is what to do:

- Rather than dropping the treat into the basket, hold it in one hand and put it to his nose.

- Place your other hand under his jaw to gently stop him from dropping the toy as you move the treat over the center of the basket.

- Then remove your hand from under his jaw and allow him to drop the toy and take the treat.

At these early stages, it's OK if the dog goes straight for the toy again after he eats the treat. That's normal. We just want to make sure that the toy drops into the basket. Give your dog lots of praise. Practice only 3 or 4 times so he doesn't get too bored or confused, then continue a few hours later or the next day.

The next step is to have your dog walk a few steps to the basket and repeat the process. Say *put away* or whatever command you've chosen and reward your dog *after* he drops the toy in the basket by tossing a treat into the basket immediately after he drops the toy.

Once he begins to understand, you can start to send the dog slightly ahead of you. Say *put away* and point at the basket. Praise when he drops the toy, so he knows he did it right. Then give the treat 5 or 10 seconds later.

"Put away your toys" might even inspire your children to do the same!

Eventually, you can start from farther away and with a greater amount of time between the basket drop and the treat, although the verbal praise should be immediate. You can even skip the treat occasionally, as long as you praise, so that your dog never knows when a treat is coming. The dog should learn, over time, that when you say *put away*, he can put toys in the basket and receive a verbal or treat reward. Once your dog truly understands the game, making the treat a random reward is actually more motivational than receiving it every time. This is a great game for children to play with their dog because kids get bored on rainy days too.

HIDE AND GO SEEK

Hide and Go Seek can be an exciting game for both dogs and their owners. It uses the smell sensors we spoke about earlier and your dog's natural curiosity coupled with his desire to be with you. It will be fun to see your dog wag his tail in excitement every time he finds you.

The game requires you to have taught your dog sit or down stay and that he can do so for at least a full minute. It also requires that your dog comes when called. We teach how to do that in *The Art of Training Your Dog,* and both Marc and the Monks offer dog training seminars if you need additional help. Alternatively, a family member can hold the dog's leash while you hide.

Start with an easy hiding spot and move on only when your dog has mastered finding you. Hide and Go Seek is also a game that you can play outdoors in pleasant weather, but it is also the perfect rainy-day game and doesn't require many steps to learn.

Tell your dog *stay* in a spot with minimal distractions. Then go hide somewhere that is out of sight but very easy to find, like just around a corner or behind a table right in front of your dog. Once you're ready, call to your dog, like "Buster, come!" Continue to call him in a happy voice until he finds you. It will happen quickly because you made it easy. Give lots of praise and a treat.

Once your dog picks up on the game, he may excitedly jump the gun and try to find you before you call him. If that happens, say nothing—no scolding, no correction, but no praise either. Quietly lead him back to his spot.

Over time, you can try progressively more difficult hiding spots, like closets or bathrooms with the door at least cracked open. Watch as your dog searches for you with his eyes and his nose. Make a big happy fuss every time your dog finds you, so he knows that you're playing a very fun game.

GO TO YOUR CRATE

We have a confession to make. Some activities are actually useful training exercises with a bit of fun built in, so the dog learns to like it from the beginning. Although we are not trying to trick the dog, it certainly helps when he *wants* to participate. Remember how Tom Sawyer convinced his friends to do the chore he had been assigned? He didn't want to whitewash the fence, so he cleverly figured out how to help others feel lucky to do it for him . . . and to pay for the privilege.

Similarly, casinos make you feel lucky to win. Every time you win a hand of blackjack or even a few coins from a slot machine, the pleasure and excitement centers in your brain are stimulated, releasing pleasurable brain chemistry. It feels good—especially if you win a big jackpot. All casino games are designed for you to win often, but also designed in such a way that you never know when the next win is coming. It could be the very next spin, or it could be eight spins from now. It will come, eventually, but you never know when or how much you'll win.

As long as a casino wins 51 times, and you win 49, they will still make a fortune because you'll keep playing, anticipating that next victory.

Dog training games work the same way. Once your dog has learned the game, you don't want to give a treat every time. You want to start adding varying time in between treats so that he never quite knows when the next treat is coming. He'll still play the game, but he won't need a treat every time to enjoy it. As long as he sometimes gets treats—or toys and praise if he isn't especially food-motivated, he'll be hooked.

You'll use these concepts with this next game, one which has the added benefit of helping your dog get more comfortable with a crate. Perhaps you taught crate training when your dog was a puppy in a way similar to what we will describe in Chapter 9 (page 155). If you didn't or if you adopted a grown dog, it's not too late. Let's start with size. The crate should be large enough for your dog to stand up without crouching, and large enough for him to easily turn around. As for type, you may choose either wire or plastic. Wire is more common and generally cheaper. Yet in our experience, we've observed that many dogs seem to prefer the more private space within a plastic crate.

Some dogs don't like the crate because they associate it with their owner leaving. Turning the crate into a rainy-day game can help. If your dog currently dislikes his crate, you may want to start with a higher value food item such as small bits of cheese, dehydrated beef liver, or the ultimate secret weapon . . . little pieces of liverwurst. If your dog is well crate-trained already, his kibble or a normal training treat will do.

Pick your preferred command to begin. Some people like the phrase *go to your house* or *go to bed*. Some people prefer to just say *crate*. Choose something you'll use consistently.

First, hold a treat that your dog likes right to his nose and, using a leash, lead him into the crate as you say the command. If you hold the leash close to his collar with your other hand, you'll simply put that hand and the dog into the crate at the same time and your treat hand tosses the treat toward the back of the crate. Don't lock the crate. Let your dog get the treat and come out at his leisure. Repeat 3 or 4 times maximum. Then stop the session. You can play two or three sessions as long as they're a few hours apart. We want your dog to look forward to the game rather than getting bored with it.

The next step is to say the command as you lead your dog into the crate as before, but without a treat in hand. The instant he's inside, fish a treat out of your pocket and toss it in the crate. Your dog will start to learn that the command means he must go into the crate but that you'll make it rewarding. To vary the game and keep it fun, you can lay a trail of treats on the floor leading into the crate, and your puppy will follow it just like Hansel and Gretel.

Eventually, you will start closing the door on your dog before giving him the treat. Before you do, start spacing out the treats. Do not give your dog a treat every time. Let him anticipate if and when a treat is coming. Like slot machine players, the dog will wait and wonder whether he'll get a treat this time. And so, he will readily enter the crate with anticipation.

Once your dog has mastered responding to this command, you can start closing the door. Wait a minute or so, then give him the treat. Eventually, you can put your dog in the crate for several minutes and elongate that over time.

Here's another reward you can add to the game as you begin to leave your dog in the crate for longer but still reasonable periods of time. Begin to keep a long-lasting chew in the crate, something your dog will consider truly special. Just don't let him remove it from the crate when you let him out. That bone is for crate time only. So, you'll have to start locking him out of the crate when you're not using it. And that has the beneficial effect of making your dog think it's a privilege to be in his crate. Remember Tom Sawyer and the fence? Alternatively, you can remove the bone and put it away if you prefer to keep the crate door open when your dog isn't in it. Either way, your dog will learn to enjoy his private time.

Learning to go to his crate means you won't have to drag your dog in there.

CHAPTER 6

Teaching Tricks with a Purpose

How to Teach Thoughtfulness
Rather Than Overexcitement

A man came to see us with his Portuguese water dog.

"How can we help you?" we asked.

"Please watch this and then I will tell you," he replied.

In an excited, motivating voice he exclaimed, "Jasmine, heel!" then proceeded to execute a complex heeling pattern of tight circles, figure eights, and constantly changing angles. Jasmine was glued to his leg the entire time, her head tilted upward to maintain constant eye contact with her owner. He stopped and looked at us. We almost clapped. But he barked the *heel* command again and repeated the entire routine. *Backward*. Again, Jasmine was perfect. Her body quivered with excitement.

After that the man ran Jasmine through an impressive routine of tricks, issuing commands in the excited tone of a circus performer.

"Bang! You're dead!" he said pointing to the eager dog. She fell over onto her side, head down.

"It's a miracle! You're healed!" he cried, throwing his hands into the air. Jasmine leapt to her feet and danced in circles on her back legs. Once Jasmine and her owner ran out of tricks, they were both panting with excitement and exertion. Yet Jasmine didn't relax. She poked and prodded the man like she wanted more.

"To be frank," we said, "In all our decades of experience, we've never seen a client with such a highly skilled dog. What can we possibly help you with?"

The man hung his head.

"When we go for a walk, she attacks people and dogs, and I can't stop her."

Teaching tricks to dogs is a lot of fun. It appeals to adults, and especially to children. In fact, the first thing many of us learned to teach a childhood dog was *give paw*. It's a classic and youthful rite of passage. Although the experience of learning together is generally valuable for both people and dogs, we might also ask ourselves at any given moment, "What lesson are we truly teaching?" One of the few certainties with dogs is that the law of unintended consequences may apply.

Jasmine's owner wanted to teach tricks to take advantage of her native intelligence, giving them a fun togetherness activity. His style of teaching was to use excitement as motivation. That seemed logical to him because Jasmine was an excitable dog, and she snapped to attention when he matched her level of frenzy.

But the more she learned, the more fidgety she became. The owner inadvertently fed her internal turmoil by failing to help Jasmine find her off switch, and by continually giving her more of what she was demanding. But what was she demanding? He thought she wanted ever more complicated tricks. But what Jasmine really wanted was overstimulated, adrenaline-fed excitement. Much the way a gambling addict can become hooked on a specific brain chemistry, so too had the dog become addicted to overstimulation. Since she had no way to turn that off, each time she became excited on a walk, her brain would flip into overstimulation mode. Because she was held back with the leash, overstimulation instantly converted to frustration at the restraint. Like a series of dominoes falling at the speed of light, Jasmine quickly began to lose control each time she encountered people and dogs while walking in the city. Naturally this worried the owner, who soon became nervous when walking his dog. As bonded as she was to him, we're sure Jasmine could sense his concern every time they approached others, and thus the constant attacks intensified in a vicious cycle.

Although Jasmine was an unusually acute case, still, when we teach tricks, we should take the dog's frame of mind into account at any given time. Excitement and intelligence, channeled into a structured tricks routine, will yield a dog who is eager to perform for treats and attention. But let's include the off switch we will discuss in Chapter 8 (page 135), so your dog can not only enjoy exciting activity, but also learn to relax and enjoy normal, rejuvenating down time. It's easy to do. If you have a dog who pesters you to do tricks, just ask for a moment of relaxation first. The classic example is a dog who has learned to give paw for praise and treats, but who now paws at you constantly hoping for that reward. Rather than scolding—or rewarding—ask for a down or a sit, then reward for that instead of for unsolicited pawing.

Still, dog tricks are a lot of fun and offer a great way to involve children in the family pet's care. As they learn to teach the tricks, family members will come to understand more about how dogs learn. Remember, how we trick train plays a big role in your dog's behavior.

Tricks That Help Behavior

It's best to use tricks to gain focus and to learn better household behaviors. If you're not mindful of behavior, you'll give the dog more attention when he's doing something wrong rather than when he's doing a good behavior. Overexcited dogs will find they get more attention when they're barking, scratching, whirling, or behaving wildly. They may earn negative attention, but that's fine with many dogs. Just like little children, dogs prefer negative attention to none.

But when we teach a dog how to earn rewards through tricks, he must settle his mind to focus on the game. We can also use tricks to guide behavior, teaching ones that will show your dog what you want him to do by naming some of the behaviors he already likes.

Labeling Natural Behaviors: Take a Bow

You can turbocharge trick training and make it easier for your dog to learn by labeling natural behaviors he already does.

Mike bought a young Sheltie named Demo and wanted to bond more by teaching his puppy new tricks. He noticed that every time Demo got up from a nap, he would give a big stretch, with his chin to the ground, his butt in the air. It almost looked like he was bowing. So, one day Mike woke Demo from his nap—and the puppy began stretching. Mike made a gesture with his hand and quietly said, "Demo, bow."

Demo, who had no idea this was a command or even a trick, finished his stretch. Mike gave him a treat and said, "Good bow, Demo!" Over the next several weeks, every time Demo woke from a nap and began to stretch, Mike repeated the same routine again, and again, and again. After a while Demo started to notice that when he stretched after Mike said "bow," he would get a treat and affection.

Then Mike tried something different. They were playing together in the living room, and Mike made the usual hand gesture and said "Demo, bow." Then he waited. At first, Demo seemed confused, because he was not waking up from a nap. But then he tried a tentative and smaller stretch. Mike ignored the fact that it was less "stretchy" than normal and rewarded as usual, giving credit for the effort.

Was Demo actually bowing to his owner? No. He was stretching. But by labeling the behavior as a "bow," Mike made it look like Demo was bowing to him, and Demo was learning that a stretch on command would get him praise and reward.

This is called "labeling the behavior." We isolate a behavior that your dog naturally does, and we give it a name. The name can be the behavior itself (such as "dig") or it can be what the behavior looks like in human terms such as "shake hands." The key point is to take an existing behavior and give it a name.

All dogs have instincts that relate to some combination of their personality and breed or breed mix. For example, huskies are "handsy." They like to touch things with their paws and manipulate objects. Sometimes it seems like they're even trying to open doors that have lever doorknobs.

That's because they have been bred with an instinct to dig into snow and to hunt little creatures under the drifts like rabbits and mice. Many terriers were bred for similar hunting behavior, to dig out prey, so they have a natural tendency to use their front feet in a digging motion. Although it was useful for the purpose of these breeds, it can be really annoying when your terrier decides to dig in the carpet or tear up your garden, just like it can be upsetting when a border collie nips at children's feet, or a papillon jumps on your guests. Many of these instinctive behaviors will earn your dog a scolding instead of a praise. The good news is you can turn them into tricks performed in a more appropriate setting, so your dog can earn praise instead of a reprimand. We'll start with some easy ones and work our way up.

DANCE

By teaching tricks started with labeling, we can channel unwanted behaviors into desirable or even cute ones that we can ask for when convenient. Take the papillon or any little dog who hops around on his back feet trying to jump in your lap or begging. Technically, this is naughty behavior, but we have to admit it's cute. If we give the behavior a label, like "dance," holding a treat just above his nose and making little circles with it, the dog will stay upright longer, "dancing." Eventually the hand motion can transition into a signal telling him to start the behavior. In time, the treat can be given *after* that dance rather than during.

Not only have you taught your dog a trick, but you can also use it to show her when to engage in the behavior and when not to. She'll learn that there are times when dancing is welcomed and rewarded, but that if you didn't ask for it, it will be gently discouraged and certainly not rewarded. She still gets to be a dog, hopping around on her back legs—just at more opportune moments.

POTTY ON COMMAND

You may have already used labeling without even knowing it. Millions of dog owners have intentionally—and sometimes completely accidentally—taught their dogs to eliminate on command. When a dog is urinating, we

Dogs who like to stand on their back legs can easily be taught to "dance."

might say something like *go potty, go potty* and when the dog finishes, we say *good potty*. Eventually, as the puppy is sniffing about preparing to go, saying *go potty* will produce the desired result. Before long the dog understands that "go potty" means I should take my opportunity right now. Whatever phrase you choose, this is a super handy trick when it's raining or you're pressed for time.

That step after labeling is what we call "gentle commanding." It is more like a suggestion because the dog is not yet entirely certain of the link between the words and the behavior. With gentle commanding, we tell the dog to perform the behavior right before we expect him to do it anyway. Remember when we said "go potty" immediately before the dog urinates, while he's sniffing the spot? That's gentle commanding. Eventually your dog will understand the term you use and associate it with the behavior.

"Go potty" on command is a useful trick.

Don't pressure your dog when transitioning from labeling to gentle commanding. He is still figuring it all out. He'll pick up on the concept, but give it time. Repetition helps. This is also where the whole family can be involved. If you have a young son who is taking your dog out to eliminate, he can try this as well, so everyone is involved in the process.

Eventually, you can turn this into a real command. Say *go potty* when you're outside with your dog at a time when he should logically have to go and see what he does. If you have prepared for a couple of weeks, he will recognize what you're suggesting. Sooner or later, you'll have a dog who will go on command . . . at least when he has to. This is not only great for when you're in a hurry, but it also can help with potty training, since it will reinforce the idea that he should eliminate outside and in specific locations rather than, say, in the house or in your grumpy neighbor's yard.

Although we have discussed stretching, dance, and potty, this is how we use labeling to take almost any normal behavior and turn it into a trick. Both labeling and the next step, gentle commanding, should always be delivered in a calm, steady way, rather than with excitement or insistence. Too much eagerness and pressure will either distract or worry your dog and can actually interrupt the behavior you are trying to encourage.

DIGGING FOR GOLD

Let's talk about what we can do for the terrier or any dog who digs in your carpet. Many owners try to stop the dog from digging altogether. If you've ever had this issue, you already know you're fighting an uphill battle. The behavior reappears over and over again. That's because it's difficult to eradicate a behavior that is instinctual and that your dog actually enjoys.

But you *can* teach your dog there is a time, and especially, a place to dig. You can also teach that there are places where digging is off limits. We can do that all by labeling the behavior and turning it into a trick.

Just like in the Take a Bow example, you can be creative and give the trick a special name. You can say something like "Find Gold!" or "Escape!"

Some dogs have a favorite digging spot on the carpet. For now, cover that spot with a plush bathmat. It will be new, soft, and tempting. Ideally, you'll notice him digging at it so you can label the behavior. If he's reluctant, try hiding a treat under the edge so he is more likely to dig it out. Each time you spot your dog digging, label it with the name of the trick you selected and make a digging motion with your hands. The hand motions add to the association, so that your dog is not only learning what you say but also what you do. Dogs respond very well to hand motions, so it is useful to add those to the label.

Even when occupied, dogs are still curious about the world around them. So, while you're labeling with "Find Gold!" and making the gesture, your dog may pause to try to figure out if he's in trouble again. If that happens, briefly look away and ignore. But every time you see your dog digging, label it and make the hand gesture. Occasionally, and sometimes when he's not looking, hide a treat under that carpeted mat to maintain his interest.

Eventually, by observing your dog, you'll be able to predict when he's likely to dig, based on things like body posture. Then you start giving the gentle command right beforehand. This is the suggestion phase again. Because your dog was going to dig anyway, he still will, and you've built another association. Finally, after you've practiced for a while, you can try to give the *dig* command in other settings. In the first few weeks, reward any success heavily and ignore any failure.

Remember, this is trick training with a purpose. It is designed to teach your dog when and where you want him to dig. Once your dog knows the trick, you can start to show him where he will be rewarded for the behavior. So, if he starts digging in an inconvenient location, do not react negatively. Instead, view this as a valuable trick teaching opportunity. Interrupt the digging by (happily) calling your dog to you, whereupon you'll lay out his special digging mat and encourage with the command

and what has now become your hand signal. Once he performs the trick, reward heavily with praise and extra treats.

Here is the sequence of what you did. First, you interrupted the behavior you don't like in that location. Second, you redirected that dog to a location you do approve. Third, you rewarded for compliance. Your dog will learn that you have a preferred digging spot. Not only did you teach your dog a trick, but you also altered an unwanted behavior while still allowing him to be a dog and use his instincts.

> **Pro Tip:** If your dog has the unfortunate habit of digging holes in your yard, you can transfer this trick to what we'd call a designated digging area. You can use garden fencing to create a small approved area for this activity, or you can set up a children's sandbox and teach him to confine his excavations to that area.

GIVE PAW

We teach our dogs to sit, stay, and come. But probably the first "trick" most of us teach a dog is to Give Paw. Or you may choose a different label, like Shake Hands. This is another great trick to involve your family. Even small children love helping teach your dog to Give Paw.

Many dogs will naturally bat a paw at you if you put your hand out in front of

them. Put a hand, palm up, in front of your dog so he can easily reach it, and see if he tries to touch or swat your hand with his paw. As soon as he does, you can say the label, like Give Paw. If he's reluctant to lift a paw, touch him lightly on the back of a front paw, just below the carpal pad. That's the pad on his front foot that looks a bit like a toe, but which doesn't touch the floor or have a nail. Touch or lightly tap behind the joint under the pad as you hold your other hand out. You'll give him the idea that he should at least pick that foot up off the floor. If he does, even if he doesn't shake hands, be sure to praise the effort.

Repeat until your dog understands the label, then work your way up to a gentle command, and eventually a real command. Ultimately, your dog will learn that when your hand comes out and you say *give paw*, it's an opportunity for him to earn praise or a treat.

Here's a really useful addition to this classic trick. Some dogs tend to paw at you and your children. Once your dog has started to pick up on *give paw*, we can first use the command *sit* and then ask her to give paw. That way, she learns the only rewarding time to give paw is when she's been told to sit first.

Dogs who learn to give paw on command are likelier to use it in a charming way instead of clawing at you for attention. They're more likely to sit and offer the paw hoping for a treat rather than scratching at your guest's legs. Plus, if he becomes overexcited, as dogs will, you can focus him without reprimanding by giving him something to do that he understands.

SPEAK ON COMMAND

Excessive barking is a common dog owner complaint yet alerting the family is a natural dog behavior. They are territorial and protective by nature. Ever since dogs emerged from wolves, they have possessed the useful instinct to let people know when they hear a strange noise, sense danger, or see prey. It can be especially problematic for those who live in apartments or condos where neighbors may become upset by barking throughout the day.

You're not going to completely stop your dog from barking. Some breeds are, quite literally, bred for extra alertness. Anyone who has ever owned a Miniature

Schnauzer or Yorkie knows what we mean. Others think *better safe than sorry* and would rather alert you to potential danger than let it come to the house. If you live with this kind of dog, chances are you've already tried to teach him that not every little sound from the outside represents a full-scale invasion.

If we can't fully stop it, we *can* channel that barking, turn it into a trick, and take a bit of control over his verbal expression. By labeling and teaching him how to bark on command, you can teach your dog that there is a right time and a wrong time to bark. Plus, you'll have another trick in your repertoire.

At first, you'll have to grin and bear it when your dog barks. We need him to do the behavior so we can label it. That means for a time, you'll have to stop scolding him, at least until you've labeled it and rewarded. We'll look at this as a teachable moment. The treat reward will likely interrupt the barking anyway so you may just be killing two birds with one stone.

Instead of the usual angry reprimand when he barks, give him the label, like *speak* or whatever command you find the most fun. Just make sure you're consistent, and for this trick, you'll want to start with an excited note in your voice.

When your dog barks, you follow the same process we used before. First, label it when he's barking. Then, try to do it right before he barks. Then, eventually, try to use the command at a time when she wasn't originally going to bark.

Now, the goal of this chapter is to teach tricks for fun, but also to change behaviors. In this case, you want your dog to bark less or at more opportune times. You cannot scold, but what you can do is begin to teach your dog to associate barking with other, better situations and places. You can also use this as a game.

Barking is no different from other labeled tricks. Should your dog offer to shake hands when you didn't want him to, no harm done, you just don't shake their hand, you don't reward, and you move on. When you ignore the behavior that you didn't ask for, she will begin to do it when you want her to and do it less when you don't.

The same is true of barking. If she barks when you don't want her to, after she has thoroughly learned the *speak* command, you can calmly tell her *quiet* and don't reward her. Then, later, you can give her the *speak* command and reward. Again, we interrupt what we don't like, redirect to something we prefer, and then we reward for that.

ROLL OVER

We prepare for Roll Over in stages. This trick is a little easier to teach if your dog already knows the *down* command. In this case, ask your dog to lay down and help him onto his side. Place a treat on the floor right at his nose and let him eat it. Repeat regularly but not so often that your dog gets bored. He'll quickly learn that it is rewarding to lay on his side.

Once he knows this step, lay him on his side, putting the treat to his nose as usual, but roll it slightly up and away from him in a circular motion. You're moving it slightly up and around his head, toward the floor on the other side of his head. If you keep it quite close to his nose, maybe an inch upward and roll it away from him as described, he will be tempted to either roll *himself* toward the treat or at least adjust himself to stretch toward it. Reward either of these moves by giving the treat because he is making an effort.

Slowly and over time we ask for more and more movement before we release the treat. Eventually your dog will realize he has to lay down on his side and quickly roll over to earn the treat. That rolling circular hand motion you used early on will become your hand signal for this trick as well as verbally saying *roll over*! We recommend you introduce the verbal command once your dog is close to completing all the steps, and this is a trick where adding a bit of excitement to your voice may actually help your dog learn it faster.

If your dog doesn't know the *lay down on your side* command, you can teach it to her by labeling it every time she voluntarily assumes the position. Say *side* each time she does so, until she can do that step, earning the initial treat. Then proceed from there. By the way, *side* is a useful "trick" all by itself, because you can use it when you want to clip nails on that side, then *roll over* to get the other side.

Get Your Dragon—Naming Your Dog's Toys

Believe it or not, it is entirely possible to teach your dog the difference between each of his toys by naming them. With this trick, your dog learns to fetch or play with a specific object by name.

Start with two toys very different in appearance from one another. An example would be a plush hot dog and a stuffed dragon. It will help if they are vastly different shades, one darker and one lighter. Another tip is to use toys that have the size and texture your dog prefers. Some small dogs love to drag big toys around but others much prefer something they can easily pick up. Begin with an understanding of your dog's preferences.

Years ago, we thought dogs saw entirely in black and white, but now we understand they see a range of color, though more limited than what we humans detect. Before you feel sorry for them though, remember that the mantis shrimp sees approximately 10 times more colors than we do! Each species has evolved with the vision they need to succeed.

Start with two favorite toys of vastly different shades, dark versus light, and very different shapes. It will be handy to start with your dog on a leash if he tends to wander away, but if he is engaged, you do not need it. Keep him by you and toss the first toy, let's say the dragon, about 4 feet away to the left. Gently hold your dog back but release him, saying, "Hot dog!" just as you throw the hot dog toy about 4 feet to the right.

If he chooses to go toward the wrong object, you may use the line to stop him *gently*. Don't be frustrated or angry, just redirect him back to the other toy as you repeat the word "hot dog."

If your dog should actually pick up the wrong object, don't react negatively, and certainly do not scold. We want to maintain his playful willingness to participate. But we want to make the game far more rewarding when he plays it your way. Silently and softly, take the wrong toy out of his mouth and try again.

"Hot dog!"

You'll make it easier at first by using only a single word name for the toy, saying "hot dog" rather than using a lot of extraneous words such as "go get your hot dog." Although you can add those words later when your dog really understands the trick, right now simplicity will help him grasp the concept that each toy has a different name and that he will be rewarded for getting the correct one.

When he succeeds, make a big happy fuss with lots of praise and affection. You may use a treat if your dog really likes them. Repeat a couple of times, then take the hot dog out of the game by putting it away so that only the dragon is visible.

Point to it and say, "Dragon!" You may need pick it up and toss it to get him interested. Once he gets the dragon, praise and reward. Then put both toys back and repeat. Or break off and come back to it again later. When teaching tricks and playing games, we always want to stop while the dog is still having fun. That way he'll look forward to next time. Short happy practice sessions—ending on a successful note—are best unless the dog exhibits a clear desire to continue.

Start this game by keeping one toy to the left and one to the right. But do mix it up when it comes to which goes left and which goes right. We don't want our puppy to think that "hot dog" is the human word for right or "dragon" is the word for left.

Pro Tip: Your dog may learn by trial and error, in which case there will be lots of errors. This is quite normal. Rather than becoming frustrated, relax, secure in the knowledge that this is part of the process. Enjoying the teachable moments makes trick training a great deal more fun. Second, some dogs will go to the toy and play with it rather than bringing directly back to you. If he goes to the wrong toy, remove it calmly as previously mentioned. But if he goes to the correct toy and plays with it rather than bringing it, give him a moment to do that. Mark the moment he selects it with praise but let him play with it for a moment if that's what he wants to do. He'll consider it an important part of the reward.

Once your dog is doing well at this stage, *place* the two objects rather than throwing them and ask him to go get one you select. Point at it to make the job easier. When he does it, praise and reward, but this time put it back in the position, rather than remove it from the game. Again, a leash will be handy for dogs who don't wait for you to tell them which one you want. You can gently keep such a dog near you, so he doesn't run to a toy before you've directed him. If he's enthusiastic though, that's good. We don't want to discourage that enthusiasm. We want to maintain and focus it.

MARKING THE MOMENT

Some dogs may benefit from a marker that tells them they have made the right selection at the exact moment they do so. Your marker can simply be the word *yes* spoken in a happy quick tone so he knows you're happy with his choice. If the dog goes to the hot dog when you ask and looks uncertain about whether he should pick it up, you'll say, "Yes!" He will feel confirmed in his choice and will commit to the activity with greater pleasure. Conversely, if he goes to the wrong toy and looks at you questioningly, maintain a neutral face as you dramatically point to the other one. When he goes there, mark the moment even if he doesn't pick it up. Baby steps to success are still steps in the right direction and the first step is knowing which toy has which name.

Once your dog has mastered this, you can have your dog get the dragon first, then the hot dog. Eventually, you can introduce a third toy. One border collie was reputed to know dozens of toys by name. But not every dog has to be a genius in that way. It's still very impressive to have a dog who can distinguish between his hot dog, dragon, and pineapple.

This trick is also interesting because it can morph into other tricks and games. For example, once your dog knows what a "dragon" is, you can then work on "find your dragon," sending him to find it out of sight. That combines Find Your Toy, a game we introduced in Chapter 5 (page 87), along with this name game.

LABELING AND GENTLE COMMANDING CAN HELP

Even if you're not working on this trick, but you notice your dog picking up or playing with his hot dog, it's a good time to say the word. That's labeling because he's already doing the behavior and you are telling him what it's called. And when you notice he is about to pick up the dragon, say the word. That's gentle commanding because you have made the suggestion an instant before he was going to do it anyway. These concepts help your dog grasp the names for these toys.

FADING THE DRAMATIC POINTING

In the early phases of this trick, we use the name of the toy, and we point at it simultaneously and in a very obvious manner. As time goes on, however, we will begin to point less and less obviously, especially as we sense the dog begins to learn the actual names of the toys. Eventually you won't point at all, but it will help give your dog a hint if you *look* at the toy you have just named.

Early on in this book, we made mention of our view that the dog is a complex problem-solving predator. Their natural abilities and native intelligence give them a lively mind. You and your dog will enjoy one another even more if you teach him a few tricks. Most dogs enjoy showing off for guests, and that will give them something better to do than jumping on company. Remember to incorporate downtime and off-switch activities into your tricks routine so that your dog not only enjoys the rush from his tricks routine but also learns the pleasure of relaxation.

CHAPTER 7

Agility at Home

How to Play with Basic Equipment

The sport known as Agility dates back only to 1978 but has quickly grown into one of the best known and most loved dog activities for both hobbyists and competitors. The most important annual dog show in the United Kingdom is sponsored by The Kennel Club and is called Crufts. The show is televised, much like the Westminster Kennel Club in New York City, and it draws a large audience in person as well as in the media. In 1978, the Crufts organizers wanted to showcase dogs doing an exciting and fun performance for their global audience.

Maybe due to the United Kingdom's heritage of steeplechase horse events involving jumps and obstacles in a timed event, the show coordinators arranged for a similar spectacle but for dogs running a complex course under the direction of the owner. Similar to a rider guiding a horse, dog and owner enter the show ring together. The owner then directs her dog over and through a variety of challenges. The dog and human team are judged on time and form. That first exhibition took place in 1978 at Crufts but quickly spread to the Unites States where it is now a sanctioned American Kennel Club event for purebreds and mixed breeds alike. It is so popular that agility clubs and classes have been organized throughout the United States and a host of other countries.

Because of its popularity, our clients frequently ask about the value of agility as a way to help their dogs get exercise and to have an activity they can do together. We believe agility can have a valuable place in life with your dog. That's because it teaches controlled excitement, a commitment to not only moving the body fast and furiously but simultaneously thinking about and obeying the rules in order to receive a qualifying score. The highest-level athletes, regardless of the sport, not only move their bodies but also use their minds to both literally and figuratively stay in bounds. And that is what the team must do in agility. That's because the ring will be filled with challenges such as hurdles, a tunnel, a table to hop onto, weave poles, and more. The dog must take the obstacles in the order assigned by the judge.

This chapter will focus on how to create your own playground at home using some Agility equipment and teaching the skills to your dog so he can enjoy them. This is not quite the same as competitive Agility. It's more like teaching a child to shoot hoops on his own backboard versus coaching him for the NBA.

There are some informal prerequisites for taking Agility formal classes that you should understand. Remember, these are group events. Although most dogs will be leashed when not practicing, dogs will be off leash on and off throughout the class. So, the dogs who typically enjoy Agility classes have high energy levels and are accepting of other dogs. We recall one client who said, "My dog loves Agility but he runs the course wildly and does what he wants out there instead of taking my guidance on the order of things. Worse yet, sometimes he runs right out of the course and won't come back!"

Learning to traverse obstacles . . .

. . . often leads to a more confident dog.

Agility class is not the place to teach obedience commands such as come when called. You'll want to be ready for that before you jump too far down the Agility rabbit hole. Preparing so your dog can take direction from you at key moments will help you a lot as you and your dog begin this exciting sport. If you pay special attention to the recall games in Chapter 3 (page 43), you will probably enjoy your foray into Agility even more.

Cyndy Douan is a professional dog trainer, Agility instructor, and a highly accomplished competitor. She has won more than 150 Agility titles with breeds as diverse as pugs, golden retrievers, and border collies, running through complicated obstacle courses in record times. She describes the sport as a "dance of energy."

She says, "In Agility you use your words and your body to signal to the dog what you want at any moment. So, it really is like a moving dance of energy. You draw the dog into your mind . . . you make a connection with him. When it all comes together, and you get that perfect, beautiful run, it's zen-like and the dog feels it too."

Cyndy recommends formal classes or even backyard agility practice for people who want to make their energetic dog happy. "People turn to agility even more for their dogs than for themselves," she notes. "Although it is beneficial for people too, most owners really want to make their dogs happy by helping them enjoy this sport. But once they get going, people find the increased connection they experience with their dogs is a huge bonus."

"The beautiful thing about agility is that in so many cases it gives people the will to keep going," Cyndy continues. "They come to class with multiple sclerosis, they come from their chemo treatments, they come with canes or in wheelchairs. But they come. They run their dogs through the course, and they keep coming back because they want their dogs to be happy. I remember an overweight man who came to my class. He

wanted to learn Agility with his dog and this desire changed his life and made him healthier. He had gastric bypass surgery and lost weight so that he could do Agility with his dog. The people come in whatever form and condition they can. They come with a desire to play with their dogs, and they fight through the challenges because the love of the dog keeps them going."

This chapter will help you get started with a few pieces of typical equipment so you can play structured games at home in the backyard. You can purchase the equipment from online stores or from the large ecommerce sites that sell books and general merchandise. You will also find information on how to build your own with items from the hardware store. Those who want to become serious competitors at sanctioned Agility trials should consult a local trainer or club in order to learn competition rules and techniques right from the beginning. On the American Kennel Club's website, AKC.org, you can learn more about formal Agility competition, local clubs, obstacle requirements/design and regulations. Although there is more than one organization sponsoring competitions, this will be a good start, and when we refer to obstacle requirements, we'll use the AKC rules for our examples. This chapter is not meant to replace those resources, but rather to help you enjoy Agility as play with your dog and the equipment if that is your main goal.

Also, you're not left out if you live in a city or dwelling without a backyard. The sport of "dog parkour" is sometimes called "urban agility," and we'll tell you a bit about that too. You won't need a yard or even regulation equipment. In this sport, participants teach their dogs to use items found in the neighborhood such as park benches and retaining walls.

We'll get you started with this exhilarating activity right at home or in your neighborhood. The first step with each piece of equipment is to familiarize your dog with it, to show him how to use it and then, eventually to use it with speed. You can begin many of these steps with puppies, slowly accustoming them to the nature of the gear, so that as they get older, they have already developed a comfort level. Whether with a puppy or an adult, take your time and go slow, gradually assisting your dog to a sense of confidence with each piece. When Agility play is taught artfully, timid dogs learn more confidence and bold dogs learn to blow off steam in a healthy way.

The Tunnel

The agility tunnel is made of flexible material that forms a large tube, 10 to 20 feet long. It can be shaped as a straight-through run but can also be positioned in a curve. It is much easier to start teaching your dog to run through a tunnel when he can see from the entrance all the way through to the exit. It's also useful to start with the tunnel collapsed as much as possible so that it is shortened to a minimal distance. Because the tunnel is made of material connected to a series of ribs, it can be compressed, elongated, and shaped, depending on your needs.

- Start with the tunnel compressed to its shortest distance and laid out in a straight line so your dog can see through it.

- For the first few days, let him get used to the tunnel. He'll want to sniff it and you can toss a few treats a few inches inside to see if he'll investigate.

- If your dog is confident and unafraid of the tunnel, hold his flat collar as you guide him toward the tunnel entrance at a run.

- Start only a couple of feet away so the approach will be quick.

- Don't hold him back if he wants to go in! Let go of the collar as he enters the tunnel.

- As he enters the tunnel, you'll run alongside it to the exit to encourage him through.

- With any luck, he'll beat you to the exit in which case praise him effusively and reward with treats. Or you can reward with a favorite toy.

Do allow a few days of introduction for a timid dog during which you let him sniff the equipment, take a treat from the entrance, or enter it on his own volition. But if he remains worried about the tunnel or wary of it, we'll offer a different approach than above after those first few days of patient preparation.

- Have a helper kneel down right at the mouth of the tunnel and gently start feeding the dog into the entrance.

- Meanwhile, you have gone to the exit of the tunnel.

- Kneel there and look into the tunnel so your dog can see you.

- Clap your hands and call your dog to you with happy tones to help him overcome any worry.

- Praise and treat heavily when he emerges.

- You'll always praise for effort, but these first few times through the "scary tunnel" you'll praise and treat extra and in especially happy tones to help him get over his initial concerns.

Once your dog is running through the tunnel and meeting you happily on the other side, it's time to extend the tunnel a little bit. Repeat the above processes. Every day you can extend the tunnel a foot or two, depending on your dog's confidence level. If he suddenly becomes reluctant, go back a few steps and teach him again. He'll come around and regain his confidence even as the tunnel gets longer.

As your dog gains experience running the tunnel, shorten it up a bit and add a very gentle curve. Run down to the exit as soon as he enters, so you can encourage him along. This time, he won't have a full view of daylight on the other side and hearing your voice just out of sight will encourage him forward. With time and practice, you'll eventually be able to extend the tunnel to its full length and add curves in either direction.

The Dog Walk

This obstacle looks like an elevated bridge with a ramp on both ends. The first ramp allows the dog to run up so that he can cross the center section bridge and then run down and off the second ramp. In regulation Agility, each of the three pieces—two ramps and the center bridge section—are only 12 inches wide and 12 feet long. The center bridge section will be 4 feet off the ground.

Dogs are meant to run fast up the on ramp, fly across the center section, and run

A focused husky on the Dog Walk.

hard off the down ramp. It is truly impressive to see how a confident and well-balanced dog can speed up, across, and down the Dog Walk in mere seconds. Although the dog is moving fast, he must not jump on or off the obstacle's ramps. He must run up and down so that his feet make contact with the ramps near the ground. This is a running and balance exercise, not a jumping one.

Commercially available Dog Walks come in a variety of sizes, however, to allow for teaching puppies and dogs on wider, lower surfaces. And of course, you can make your own based on easily available plans. If you are playing with Agility for fun, rather than formal competition, we recommend you use wider dimensions and lower heights for safety reasons. You and your dog can have just as much fun with an obstacle that is 2 feet wide and 2 feet off the ground as with one that is much narrower and higher. Again, as with all obstacles, but especially in this case, you want to use sturdy equipment that is firmly in place on dry ground so that it is not rickety and likely to cause injury.

- You can start your dog on or off leash depending on how much control you need.

- If you start with a leash, eliminate it once you no longer need it.

- Start slow to build confidence and to avoid mistakes. We don't want your dog to get scared and jump off the obstacle.

- Lead your dog to the very start of the up ramp and place a treat right to his nose. Some dogs will want to go up even without a treat.

- Use very small treats that can be instantly consumed.

- Center the treat in the middle of the ramp so your dog will center himself by following the treat.

- Lead him up the ramp using the treat. Give it to him at the top of the first ramp.

- A confident dog will likely be unafraid so you can lead him across the center section, then down the off ramp, or produce another treat to help guide him across.

- You'll walk alongside the down ramp as your dog goes down. Match his pace.

- Pause at the bottom of the off ramp, while he is still on it, and give several treats in rapid succession. Hold those treats very low, as if your dog is eating off the end of the ramp itself. That will help him learn to not jump off, but eventually to run off instead.

- If your dog is not confident, then break this job into multiple steps: First ramp. Center section. Second ramp. Work on only one at a time, reward and start over. Move slowly and only add a new step when your dog feels good about the previous one.

Bella (top) and Valerie (middle and bottom) help their dogs up, across, and down the Dog Walk.

Once he's got the idea and looks forward to moving all the way through the Dog Walk, you can begin walking faster to encourage your dog to pick up speed following the treat. Eventually you'll run alongside, and you won't need to produce a treat until the very end. Once your dog is predictably successful, you can substitute happy praise and encouragement during and immediately after the Dog Walk. You won't need to treat every time, just sometimes on a random basis.

Weave Poles

This obstacle is a game in which the dog runs through a line of poles inserted into the ground, rapidly weaving back and forth between them from the first pole through the last. In a formal Agility competition, there will be between 6 and 12 poles placed 24 inches apart. Often the poles are made of PVC pipe and are 40 inches

high. But if you are playing Agility games at home for fun rather than formally, you can use driveway snow stakes, provided you can push them into the ground. You can also buy or make a practice set of Agility weave poles. These often have a long metal dart at the bottom of the pole that makes it easy to push them into the lawn, but which prevents them from being too rigid if your dog should hit them when weaving between them at top speed.

This game looks deceptively simple, but there are a number of steps to show your dog how to play. Take your time with the steps to keep the practice light and fun.

Familiarize your dog with the poles by encouraging him to walk through them with a treat.

- We'll start with six weave poles laid out in a straight line, 2 feet apart, so we have a 12-foot-long obstacle.

- Starting with the second pole, move every other one a foot to the left from its original location. Once you've done that, you have two parallel lines of poles with a 1-foot gap or channel between them.

- Place your dog on a leash and walk him briskly through the channel. You'll stay on the outside of the poles, walking your dog quickly through that channel in the middle.

- Keep your dog on whatever side you normally walk him so that he better understands what is expected.

- Hold your leash a bit upward so it doesn't hit the poles and leave only a bit of slack in it so your dog doesn't feel leash pressure but it's obvious where he should go.

- Once you reach the end, give a treat.

- Repeat multiple times over the next few days so that your dog knows what to do and looks forward to trotting through the gap between the two lines of poles. Once he's comfortable and knows what to do, you can take off the leash and practice another few days off leash. You'll still treat quickly after the last pole.

Once the above steps are easy and your dog knows what to do, looking forward to that treat at the end, you're going to move the poles slightly closer together. To do that, leave your original line of poles in place, but you're going to move the line that you had placed a foot apart from their original position. Move them just a few inches closer to the first line of poles than they were before. That will close up your gap just a little. Run your dog through the channel as before, but this time he'll get used to a slightly narrower space through which to move. Once that's easy, move them again so the gap is as narrow as possible but still allows your dog to move through it.

Now that your dog has progressed to this stage, we will place all the poles in alignment, just as they first were when we placed them. Pull up the first pole, lean it substantially to the left, and push it back into the ground in the same spot as before. Pull up the second and replace it, leaning to the right, and continue down the line alternating each weave pole. Once you've finished, if you stand in front of the first pole

If your dog becomes confused, you can put the leash back on to help guide him. Then remove the leash again.

facing down the line toward the last one, that first pole be on your left, leaning left. The next pole will be on your right, leaning right, alternating all the way. The gap or channel has now become the pointy end of a "V."

Place your dog back on a leash so you can help guide him straight down the line just the same as you have done so many times before. But this time, due to the slanting configuration of the poles, he'll have to slightly adjust his trajectory to weave through without hitting them. The adjustment he has to make is very slight, so he won't worry about it at all. Most dogs take to this quickly if they have been prepared with the prior steps.

As your dog gains confidence over the next few days, reset the weave poles, just slightly decreasing the angle of lean, making them a little more vertical. Use a leash if needed, but by now you may simply be able to run alongside your dog as he bobs and weaves down the line. He's done it many times before over the last couple of weeks, slowly learning to weave his way along, but now he has to do a bit more work to dodge back and forth.

Should your dog get confused at any stage, put him back on the leash, so you can cheerfully guide him on how to move his body. Then praise and treat as he weaves through the last pole. As he begins to show precision, you can help him add a bit more speed by running down the line as he goes, trying to beat him to the end, where he gets his treat. Do not progress beyond this step until your dog is very accustomed to how we play this game. Then you can take the poles that aren't quite vertical yet and make them perfectly upright and expect the same weave as before while you run alongside.

Every dog is different. Some will master the weave poles in a few short weeks. Others might take a few months. Let your dog set the pace and don't move ahead to a new step until the previous one has gotten easy.

The Table

In Agility, the dog and handler run through multiple obstacles as fast as they can while still maintaining control, so that neither will commit an infraction that causes a penalty. At some point during the course, the dog is directed to hop up on the table for a brief pause. That the dog can jump on the table shows he is agile. That he can briefly pause there shows he is under the handler's control and not running wildly. Even though he is excited, he is willing to take direction.

We include the table here because it can have multiple uses even when you're not playing. For example, many owners find their dog is easier to groom when he is slightly elevated because he is likelier to hold still. Plus it's easier on your back. Just ask any professional groomer!

- Every platform you practice with should be stable and not tippy, especially if your dog is nervous about new surfaces.

- Start with your dog on leash. Hold a treat to his nose and lead him onto a low platform as you say *table*.

- If your dog already knows the *place* command, you might prefer to say *place*. Eventually he'll learn that whatever you're pointing as you say the word will be the place for him to jump onto.

- Give him the treat as soon as he has hopped onto the platform.

- Once he gets good at it, you can delay giving the treat until he has already hopped up.

It really is that simple, but here are a few variations that will make the obstacle more interesting for you both.

- Although you should start with a lower platform, you can introduce slightly higher tables or surfaces as you progress.

- A good rule of thumb for a jump height is no greater than one and a half times your dog's height at the shoulder blades.

- You will find some dogs are more athletic than others. They can easily jump greater heights with minimal effort. Others need lower heights.

- For safety, use nonskid surfaces.

- Don't use the kitchen table, or you may find uninvited company for dinner!

Teach your dog to wait on the table until you are ready to release him. In competitions, the dog won't be up there long, only a few seconds. But if you plan to brush your dog or clip his nails on the table, it's best to teach him to wait there and even to sit or lie down when you ask.

Urban Agility

Not to worry if you don't have a suburban backyard to store and spread out Agility equipment. You can learn to use the benches and items you'll find in public parks. Even chairs and low retaining walls can make good obstacles to teach your dog using some of the same principles we have discussed above. Public playgrounds have teeter totters and merry go rounds that some people use as part of an Urban Agility obstacle course where dogs are permitted.

Begin to look around your neighborhood for publicly accessible, dog-friendly areas featuring objects you can teach your dog to safely climb, walk over or jump on. Even boulders and railroad ties can be used to teach balance and coordination. You'll find a great deal more information at the website for the International Dog Parkour Association, www.dogparkour.org. There you'll find resources for hobbyists and competitors alike who use the environment as a sort of natural obstacle course.

Agility, whether at home or in the neighborhood, can turn the world into your dog's playground. Together, as you learn to use the obstacles, you'll become a team focused on this athletic and exciting sport. For inspiration, you might want to watch a few videos of dogs thrilled to run the course, coached by their owners. You'll see border collies flying at the speed of light, up over and across the Dog Walk, dodging through the weave poles in seconds, and diving full force into the tunnel. You'll see Great Danes working their way through the same obstacles, their size slowing them down a bit, but moving with the same dedication. You'll even see chihuahua's speeding as fast as their little legs can carry them, loving Agility as much as the big dogs. People come to Agility to help their dogs become happier and more confident. But as any Agility teacher will tell you, it ends up doing the same for the people.

CHAPTER 8

Games That Teach an "Off Switch"

We humans lead busy lives. Demands from work, family, and chores consume much of our time. That's why we sometimes want to turn off our minds and bodies to just relax.

Dogs like a bit more action. Snoozing isn't particularly attractive to energetic dogs. They already spend much of their time napping when we are not home. And they are not faced with the emotional drain of bills and responsibilities. Dogs want to have fun. In fact, they require physical and mental stimulation to thrive, and that's why fun for a dog so often looks wild and jumpy to us.

A good owner provides needed activity for the dog that is fun and engaging but, in some situations, *your* need is for your dog to take a break from the play. The easiest dogs to live with are those who voluntarily choose to relax at logical moments, even in exciting circumstances. Assuming their needs have been met, they can "read the room" and see that relaxation is the most logical choice at key moments. Such dogs will then actually choose to sit or even lie down and chew a bone without getting over-energized by the world around them.

We dog trainers call this an "off switch." The off switch is the ability of your dog to turn off his excitement and self-calm. Although some dogs seem to be born with the ability to turn off the world and relax at logical moments, it is more probable that you will have to help your pet learn this concept. Still, it is well worth helping your dog develop his off switch. It is an invaluable skill, one that can do the following:

- Keep your pet safe.

- Help your pet relax.

- Protect people and objects.

Like young children, dogs love to have fun, and this may take the form of reacting (and even overreacting) to every noise and bit of movement they can detect in and outside of the home. It can be difficult to calm your pet down without confining her. Active dogs and breeds often struggle without an off switch. They're always ready and raring to go when it's time to play games, train, or walk, but when it's time to settle down, these dogs typically struggle.

In this chapter, our goal is to help your dog develop the off switch that will help her relax when that is what you need. We want to increase her ability to settle down even when there is excitement all around. We also want to enable her to do so when it's convenient for you and your family.

What Does the Off Switch Look Like in Action?

Almost all dogs will develop some form of calming as they age. They'll learn there are situations when it is more sensible for them to just relax. But it is still important for your dog to teach her to relax on command for several reasons.

First, while dogs do tend to mellow as they get older, the "playful stage" can last anywhere from 2 to 5 years depending on the individual, breed, and personality. That can be a long time to wait for your dog to relax.

Second, even older dogs tend to rest at times that are convenient for them, not necessarily for you. Although they usually mellow with age, older dogs may become excitable when overstimulated. For example, when visitors arrive, dogs of any age may still want to jump on your guests.

Third, dogs do not always know how to stop overreacting. As humans, we know that we can slow the mind by reading a book, doing yoga, or meditating. Dogs typically don't learn many ways to relax or self-calm on their own, especially since their interactions with us usually serve to rile them up and actually reward excitement.

Opposite page: *Dogs can learn to self-calm if we teach them to relax.*

Games that teach an off switch, which we'll learn in this chapter, ultimately give your dog more controlled emotions. Don't be surprised if she begins to volunteer to rest on a dog bed, let herself into her crate, or ignore the world to enjoy chewing on a bone. The play that you'll teach her now will give her future options for relaxation—and will make it easier for you to encourage her to engage in those activities on command.

Nevertheless, it is important to remember that sometimes dogs will invent games that you don't want them to play. Marc once worked with a border collie named Rocky. Rocky was the terror of the neighborhood. His family lived on a corner lot, and Rocky was allowed to play outside as much as he wanted. He never left his yard because an underground electronic fence kept him within the confines of the property. But as far onlookers knew, he was roaming free.

A bike path ran around the perimeter of the yard, and directly behind the property was a lake. Rocky invented a game that he thought was great fun. He would hide in the bushes. When a biker came down the path, riding next to the lake, Rocky would jump out from behind the bush and chase the biker, barking and growling viciously.

Naturally, bikers could not see the electronic fence. To them, this dog was running straight for them ready to attack. More than a few riders panicked and fell into the lake trying to escape Rocky, who was acting like a rabid dog.

Rocky had the time of his life scaring these bikers until they went for an unintended swim. But it also was causing problems for the neighborhood. Marc found that Rocky's problem was a combination of an overactive "play drive" combined with boredom. Dogs who aren't given productive games to play—games with rules—are likely to invent their own amusements, and those will likely be ones that humans will not like.

Since Rocky clearly loved to chase, Marc taught him a disciplined game of fetch. In the beginning, it was a more typical form of retrieve, where Rocky would sit, Marc would throw, and Rocky would retrieve the object. Sometimes, Marc would even hide the object to make the game more fun.

The original goal was simply to give Rocky an alternative activity to use his creative energy and have fun without potentially drowning any bikers. But Marc noticed that this game also had an unintended side effect: it helped Rocky find his off switch.

When left to his own devices, and his own dangerous game, Rocky was an unsettled dog. He fit the description of a nervous or even anxious dog. If he was confined to the house, he would find an escape route. Eventually, Rocky chewed through the screen door so often, that the owners stopped repairing it. Rocky had drilled his own dog door. In out. In out. Barking. Screaming from the lake. This was how Rocky passed every day.

But in Marc's care, learning other complex but far more productive games, Rocky began to relax when not specifically engaged. Marc noticed that Rocky quickly became not only more obedient, but that the anxiety had melted away to the point that Rocky began to nap all on his own accord when his presence was not needed. Marc on the couch reading, noticed that Rocky would lay down and sleep in a corner of the room. If Marc got up to leave the room for a moment, Rocky opened an eye, but if he was not summoned with his name or a hand signal, he simply closed his eyes again to continue the snooze. The turn-around was remarkable.

Rocky was not only better behaved, but he was also far more content.

Too often, we respond to an excitable dog by unintentionally creating even more excitement, such as trying to physically or verbally calm them down. Usually this means we scold the dog. Loudly. If a dog is barking unnecessarily and you raise your voice in an attempt to quiet him, aren't you *both* barking? Sometimes we take the dog out of the situation by putting him away in a room or outside. And although that may temporarily solve the problem, in the long term it leads to more boredom and frustration and a vicious cycle of cause and effect for bad behavior.

Instead of this approach, you can teach your dog an off switch by playing games that show him he can easily shift from excitement to calm when appropriate. And in fact, that he can do so of his own volition, which we call self-calming. This is perhaps the most valuable skill of all. And that is what these games teach.

RED LIGHT/GREEN LIGHT

Most of us are familiar with Red Light/Green Light. It's a classic childhood game, one that is played in schools and playgrounds all over the world. One child yells *green light* and all the other children run around. But if they yell *red light*, everyone has to freeze in place.

Many elements make this game entertaining for young children. It is an activity where, for a few moments, they're going wild, running as fast as they can. Then suddenly, they have to stop in their tracks, moving nary a muscle to avoid being called out.

This pattern of going wild, freezing, going wild, and freezing again is what makes the game fun. It's also what makes it such a great learning experience for dogs.

To play Red Light/Green Light with your dog, your dog will need to know the *sit* or *down* command. If she's not consistent with it, you can still play, but calmly integrate the training into the appropriate moments. For dogs who are not yet solid on *sit* or *down*, it will be helpful to put a leash on your dog, although you won't hold it.

For the purpose of starting your dog on the game, we'll use the *sit* command because it is a bit easier for most dogs than the *down*, but eventually you might find the *down* leads to a better conclusion.

You have the option to use a *green light* command, or *let's play*! Say it in an excited tone and then begin to do all the typical things that humans do to rile up dogs. You can jump up and down. You can run in a circle. You can squeak a puppy toy. You can act silly. Whatever it is that gets your dog animated and excited will work.

Let your dog enjoy the fun and excitement for a few moments. He'll run around and happily get silly with you. And fairly quickly, many dogs will begin to jump on you. That is the perfect moment for Red Light to stop the action, so, in a commanding but not unkind tone of voice, say *down*.

It is normal if your dog doesn't even react to the command in this scenario. He may be so excited that he doesn't even hear you. Plus, it's very difficult for an excited dog to follow a command to hold still. But this is why we have the leash. Immediately after saying "Down," take the leash in your right hand and slide your left hand down until you're holding the leash near your dog's collar. This way you'll have much better and gentler control than if you hold the leash only by the handle. Without a leash, you may be tempted to grab your dog by the collar, but if you do that, neither of you will have much fun. Using the leash, gently help him into the down position. Once he's there, give him a treat by laying it right between his front paws to reinforce the down. Make sure he stays down by stepping on the leash, leaving plenty of slack.

During the "down" time, you will also need to emulate the behavior you want to encourage in your dog. Remain calm. Take deep breaths. Avoid staring at him (since this can make your dog excited) and you will want to avoid behaviors that are excitable. He'll try hard to lock eyes with you. Glance away and instead remain neutral.

Stay in this position until your dog settles into the calm. It can take a while, and that's OK. Most dogs will fidget for a few minutes when they are new to Red

Children love to play Red Light/Green Light too!

Light/Green Light. You will want to avoid the temptation to quickly jump up and down again. Eventually he'll sigh and visibly relax into the down. Once your dog seems calm, count to 10, and only then release him with a command like *OK* and then resume the Green Light activities, jumping up and down and getting your dog excited again.

After a few minutes of fun, repeat the *down* command, and repeat the resting process.

This is a game that should only be played in cycles of two or three, because you do not want your dog to get frustrated or confused in the early stages. Ironically, he may also start to get tired of the wild and crazy phase! We do want him to enjoy it, because only by going wild during the Green Light phase can he also come to recognize the meaning of the Red Light phase.

Most dogs love this game and are happy to play it multiple times a day, indoors and outdoors.

If you want to add a bit of nuance to your dog's vocabulary, say *green light* immediately before you start any activities that excite your dog, such as releasing your dog out of a *down* command. He'll quickly learn that *green light* means the fun is about to begin.

Red Light typically needs to be taught by first combining it with the *down* command as we described. But once your dog begins to understand, you can slowly start to fade the word *down*, and she should pick up on the meaning of the phrase. Many dog owners love integrating these words into the training process because they give you and your dog a secret language.

Marc used to play this game with his greyhound, Bobbi.

DROP ON RECALL

Easily, the most important command your dog will ever learn is to come when called. This is a valuable exercise that keeps your dog safer in a world full of cars and squirrels. Any time you have a chance to reinforce this tool is a worthwhile one, because while *sit*, *stay*, and *down* have value, it is *come* that will save your dog's life.

But teaching your dog to come when you call doesn't have to be boring. We can

A quiet moment with a smile can be a good reward.

make it quite fun as well, and—by doing so—keep your dog more mentally engaged so that she'll respond even better when called.

One game that helps your dog think through the exercise is called Drop on Recall.

The object is to call your dog, as you do normally. But, as she runs toward you, you'll teach her to "hit the deck" and lie down, immediately, even when she's running at full speed.

This game won't make a lot of sense to your dog at first, so we'll help her understand in easy stages. When your dog learned to *come*, it meant she should approach you as efficiently as possible. Adding this extra, unexpected element may confuse her a little at first, but once we teach it, it will change the boring recall into a game with more interesting possibilities. It's always easier to introduce a new game by taking a moment to get your dog focused on you.

The first step is to teach your dog to drop to the ground quickly *without* the *come* command.

It starts with a leash, but as your dog learns the game, you can take it off. Normally when we tell a dog to lay down, she is already stationary or even expecting a command. Rarely do we tell our dogs *down* without warning, but that's exactly what we'll teach here.

Take your dog on a walk, so she isn't looking at you and waiting for you to tell her what to do.

As you are walking forward, without warning, say *down* and—using the leash technique described in the Red Light/Green Light game—quickly help lead her to

Rewarding with a toy or treat makes Drop on Recall more fun for your dog.

the ground. Once she learns to respond, you can eliminate the leash for a greater sense of freedom. Stay right by your dog. Calmly praise and place a treat between her paws the moment she lies down, so she understands this is a very rewarding action. Some dogs appreciate toys even more than food, in which case you can use a favorite toy as a reward for the quick down. Release your dog from the down by saying, "OK" or "let's go," walking forward, and giving your dog a moment to play with her toy as a reward.

A couple of tips: Although you need to move into your dog and the leash quickly to show you want a rapid down, do this movement smoothly rather than lunging. We don't want to appear angry. Make your praise warm but calm, so your dog doesn't immediately spring up. But if she does get up before you want her to, ignore that for the moment because the first important accomplishment was that she took the down position. Although you do want to practice, don't overdo it. There is a fine line between fun and work.

You can then repeat this initial stage while walking in different areas. You can even do it in the house. Just make sure she doesn't know when the command is coming and that she receives praise and—now only randomly—treats when she drops to the floor.

Once she can drop to the down on her own as you are walking, the next step is to begin moving away from her while she is still in the down position. Give her a hand signal that tells her to stay in place, walk to the end of the leash, count to about 10 seconds, then release her by walking forward and encouraging her to come with you.

As soon as your dog has shown that she can do this successfully, you can start to teach her to drop *during* the *come* command.

Use a 15-foot leash and ask your dog to stay in place. Once you're at the other end of the line, call her toward you. As she's running and gets about halfway, move toward her in a friendly way and ask for that same rapid *down*. You'll likely need to help her do it by reach in to grasp the leash near her collar. Drop the treat between her paws, give her lots of praise, and make sure you give her a hand signal to tell her to stay while you move away, going back to the end of your leash. Eventually, you can do this without the leash and without the added help.

Over time you can extend how long she's down, and she should start to recognize that down time is calm time, no matter how excited she was prior to being called. Occasionally your dog may drop to the ground early, anticipating a command you didn't give. Don't scold, just call her again, and make sure that she isn't rewarded with any treats that time.

Use a mix of praise, treats, or toys to reward.

As your dog learns the final phases of Drop on Recall, start to change up the game a little to keep it fresh and interesting. Sometimes you'll call her out of the down. Other times, you'll walk back to your downed dog, praise or reward in place, and release her to a toy. If she already has her toy, simply call her to you and she'll bring it along with. This way she'll never know what's going to happen next, however, she will understand that she needs to think and observe.

GO TO BED

Here's a great way to give your dog a "chill out" place when you need a moment of
peace and quiet. It's an off-switch game that, like most, doubles as an opportunity
to help your dog stay safer and happier. For example, if you break a glass, you can
send your dog to her bed and she'll think it's a game while you clean up. Or if guests
are walking in the door and she's a bit too jumpy, you can send your dog to bed. This
is also a great game to teach when you want your dog on *her* bed rather than yours.
Placing her bed near yours should make this easier. Remember, you can have dog
beds located in multiple areas of the home. Finally, she'll learn how to turn off excess
excitement without feeling punished.

To play the bed game, we first need to turn it into a reward so your dog will *want*
to go to there.

It's handy to start with your dog on a leash, although that is optional because some
dogs will move more freely without it. Dogs who will cheerfully follow your hand
gestures may be fine off leash. Dogs who tend to ignore you, however, should be on
leash so you can gently use it to direct them. Begin by showing her that you're dropping a treat onto the bed. Say *go to bed*. Let her hop onto the bed to eat the treat. The

Indicate that you want her to go to her bed.

*As she learns the game, you can give the
reward after she gets there.*

Sometimes give treats but other times reward with praise.

first few times, it's OK if she jumps off shortly after. Rather than give treats by hand for this activity, we always drop them onto the bed because we want her to understand: *this is a rewarding place to be.*

Do this a few times then stop. As with most games, it's a good idea to leave your dog wanting more. In other words, quit while you're ahead and you'll get even quicker and more enthusiastic responses later. The next step is to occasionally drop a treat on the bed when your dog isn't looking, when you're not even playing the game. But two or three times daily, the dog will notice "Hey! Look! I wonder how that got there?!" and will hop onto the bed to snag the goodie. Keep it down to only two or three random times per day, but you'll be shocked how quickly and how often your dog begins to go to the bed entirely of her own volition.

Imagine you come home to find your name on a gift-wrapped box sitting on the table. You open it to find a $100 bill! You have no idea who left the box or how it got there, but you gladly pocket the money. You then go out to work in the yard. When you come back, the box is closed again. You open it and find another $100 bill. You will surely start checking that box multiple times a day! Even if it's usually empty, you will check often, hoping for another cash treat.

That's how we want to start training your dog to love her bed.

Once she understands this is a happy place, the next step is to tell your dog to go to bed *without* a treat. She will run to the bed to look for it. But in this case, you'll drop the treat on the bed *after she gets there* as a reward for listening to the command.

Once she excels at responding, the next step is to add a time component. Instead of an instant treat drop, wait 10 seconds. Once she's mastered 10 seconds, wait 30.

Over the course of a week, add time until she understands she may be waiting a while for the treat, but that she can use the opportunity to calm down.

Should she jump ship before the time is up, we have to be careful not to scold— we need the bed to be associated with happiness, treats, and relaxation—but no treat until she listens. You can use a leash to quietly guide her back onto her place rather than becoming insistent. Do this if she gets up before you release her with an encouraging word and her name.

Over time, you can make the game harder, and ultimately more useful, by introducing distractions. For example, you can start walking away and, if you notice she's about to follow you, point and tell her to go back. If necessary, use the leash to help her. Once she's been in the bed for 3 to 4 minutes, you can casually walk past the bed and drop a treat.

You are likely to find your dog frequently volunteers to play the Go to Bed game. If you didn't send her there, no need to drop a treat, and it's OK if she gets off whenever she wants. We only reinforce the rule that she should stay there until released if we asked her to go. Believe it or not, it can sometimes be a little inconvenient when your dog loves the game a little too much. For example, you want to take her out for first morning potty, but instead of going to the door with you, she jumps on the bed and won't move. Rather than scolding, you can just help her off and pick up the bed. Then put it away until you need it. She'll be even happier to see it next time.

Practical use of the bed game has many examples, such as when delivery comes to the door and you don't want the dog crowding the space. Or you can send her to bed when guests come over until her energy level settles. Your dog will need to have learned to stay there 10 minutes or so even in distracting circumstances, so take time and work up to it little by little.

Remember to play fair. Once a client called to say that her dog would not stay on the bed, even though we had taught the dog this game at training camp. We went to her home to try to figure out why her dog wasn't staying in the bed. We found the owner had a toddler who would jump on the bed with the dog, climbing on her back while throwing cereal!

There are some distractions that no dog can ignore. Always be fair to your dog.

TUG OF WAR

Everyone knows a dog who loves to play Tug of War with their owner. But what you may not know is that this is actually somewhat controversial in the dog training world. Many trainers discourage the game because they believe it can lead to problematic behaviors.

The theory goes that Tug of War rewards possessiveness. The dog learns that she can pull things like shoes or leashes away from you and that you'll pull back. For a dog, that is a lot of fun. But for the owner, it means that the dog will be grabbing her leash on walks. Dogs can also find this game overstimulating. Just like humans, dogs are competitive. They want to win. So they may pull harder and harder and harder.

Eventually, she may try so hard to win that your dog bites you by accident as she tries to tighten her grip. Although your dog may not think of it as aggression, a bite is a bite. Obviously, we would like to reduce the chances of biting rather than increasing them.

Still, we believe that Tug of War can be a great game when it is taught correctly. This activity uses a lot of energy and can truly be educational when matched with appropriate rules. So, yes, we recommend that your dog learn Tug of War if it appeals to her, but we also suggest you combine it with pauses and relaxation points, giving your dog yet another off switch that shows her the value of self-calming.

You'll want to purchase a toy that is long enough, so your dog won't nip you by accident when trying to get a good grip. We suggest a "tug toy," which typically has a handle on each end, one for you and one for your dog.

Start with a calm dog who understands the game won't begin until you give her permission. Placing your dog on an initial sit may help. Dangle the end of the toy in front of her face until she gets excited, then release her so she can start to grab it. Once she has a grip, pull gently and the game begins.

In general, you can play Tug of War the same way you would normally. It really is a great game for dogs. But, if you notice that she's starting to get a bit more aggressive with the object, we're going to integrate an off switch.

This dog has learned that the game begins with a moment of calm.

Take a high-value treat and put it to your dog's nose with one hand while you're still holding the toy with the other. When she notices the treat, tell her to *drop it*, and when she releases you can give her the treat. Dogs who love Tug of War may need a powerfully scented, extra tasty treat to drop the toy, but most will do it.

The best way to play Tug of War is to let your dog win a few times, and then you win a few times by telling her to *drop* or *leave it*, teaching your dog that, even in the middle of playing, she must release the rope and let you win. Mixing up who wins will keep the game fun for your dog. By telling your dog to drop it, you're telling her to let you win, but you reward her and can start the game again once she settles down. Show her that you do not play this game if she is leaping at you trying to steal the toy, but that you'll play when she calms herself for a moment.

Discourage your dog from playing Tug of War with any object that you did not

select for the game. If your dog picks up an object and wants to play, don't pull back or play, but put your hand on the object and say *drop*.

In many ways, Tug of War is really a drop game, because your dog naturally will love tug, but you're teaching her that—even though the game is fun—there are times to play and times to stop.

Dogs and People Need Self-Calming Techniques

Learning to self-calm is a valuable skill for most of us. Dogs and their owners both benefit from learning an off switch. Teaching your dog to relax can be useful for dog owners, who otherwise may complain that the dog is so wild she never settles down and often must be shut away. A dog who learns tranquility is happier and safer. Although we can't quite teach a dog to meditate or play relaxing music, we believe this chapter will help your dog lie happily by your side with a bone when you do.

Opposite page: *Begin tug with a moment of calm; play, but eventually ask your dog to drop the toy, then praise.*

CHAPTER 9

Training Games for Puppies

There is nothing like puppy love. Despite decades of professional dog work, even we are often disarmed by the charms of a puppy. Even the monks who founded New Skete never get tired of watching them play, inventing games that help them mature and adapt to their environment. When Marc visits the monastery, one of his first stops is the puppy kennel to see the babies. Our clients who have raised puppies from 8 weeks or so often look back nostalgically on those first weeks and months when the play was so uninhibited.

Of course, play is fun for puppies, but much more than amusement is afoot. As we mentioned in the introduction, play is instrumental in how a pup learns and adapts to the world because it takes instinctive drives and refines them. Pups bond with their littermates and then with their new owners through interactions that intensify the relationships as they're having fun. In this chapter we'll explain how to teach a young puppy to play games that he will enjoy and that prepare him for life in your home as a good dog.

Playing with Your New Pup: Think Ahead

Let's start with a few concepts that will help your puppy grow into the best friend you've been dreaming about. Think ahead. Your 14-pound rottweiler puppy may gain 100 pounds in less than a year. If you wrestle with him now and encourage him to put his front feet on your lap so you can pick him up, will you still enjoy it next year when he knocks you over like a bowling pin?

You've noticed your mixed breed intently watching your feet when you walk. So, you make a game out of it by rapidly shuffling them in front of his nose. His baby puppy growls and tiny little bites are adorable when you turn your anatomy into a game of "footsie." Yet countless clients have asked us to help them stop what eventually evolves into a painful "surprise attack footsie game" with an adult dog who bites them and their children hard.

We've already explained the dangers of using a laser pointer with adult dogs, but you've seen a video of cats being entertained by chasing a laser pointer dot on the floor and up the walls. It occurs to you that your puppy might enjoy the same game, and you find he does. But there are important psychological differences between cats and dogs, and one of them relates to the way they interpret chasing lights that cannot be caught. The cat typically moves on when the game is ended. But many dogs have a hidden trigger that can eventually be fired off by this game. Later, as adults, you could find them obsessively pouncing on any glint on the floor, staring for hours at a moving ceiling fan, or neurotically following shadows all day within the house.

Rather than playing games that will cause problems later, let's focus on activities that will help us raise a puppy who grows into a well-adjusted, happy, and polite dog. Before we jump into the specifics of how to do that, here are some suggestions that will help you get there easier.

- Include short periods of play throughout the day rather than one giant play session that ebbs and flows. Puppies tire out quickly and, when overstimulated turn to biting as if they were little piranhas. Ten to twenty minutes is ideal, depending on age.

- Frequent naps in the crate will help your puppy recuperate energy expended during play and the enormous amount of energy spent on rapid growth. Get your puppy on a nap schedule just like you would with a baby. This will help with crate and potty training.

- Take your puppy outside to eliminate immediately after a nap. Afterward is the perfect time to play with him because you won't have to worry about an accident.

- Try to have visitors to your home so your puppy meets a variety of people in his formative months.

- Short daily car rides will help keep your puppy from becoming carsick and worrying in the car. Drive around the block a few times on a regular basis.

Puppies play hard but they don't volunteer for naps. Be sure to create frequent rest times.

- As soon as your pup is cleared by the vet, begin to explore the neighborhood so the puppy will be used to the scents, sounds, and sights of your environment. You can keep him far from scary, noisy things like trash trucks and elevated trains, but let him slowly get used to their presence.

It is important to socialize your puppy so that he will be accustomed to people, dogs, and the neighborhood. But there are some challenges. Puppies who are not fully vaccinated are vulnerable to parvovirus and distemper. They can come into contact with both of these illnesses in areas frequented by other dogs. Follow veterinary advice about when your puppy can safely take short neighborhood walks, sniff the grass, and begin meeting other puppies. You may have to get creative to start social-izing a puppy who has not yet had all his boosters. Some trainers and day cares offer puppy socialization sessions in sterilized safe rooms. And you can take the pup, keeping her on a leash, to friends' houses from time to time to broaden her world.

Since we've established that play is an essential part of life with a dog, it makes sense to teach your pup games that are both fun and educational, which enhance your relationship. So where do we start? What we'd like to do in the rest of this chap-ter is give you some concrete games to play with your pup as well as guidelines on how to conduct them in a clear and mutually enjoyable way. Remember to start out in an undistracted area. Keep your sessions short and always upbeat. It's important not to put too much pressure on a young pup and certainly not to scold him if he doesn't do everything right. Be patient and have faith in the process.

Fetch Is the Perfect Game for Puppies

Puppies are alert, curious, and orally fixated. They explore their new world by sniff-ing and picking up everything they possibly can. That is both good news and bad news. The good news is that the average puppy can quickly learn to retrieve an object and bring it right back to you. He wants to pick up everything anyway, so really the only trick is teaching him to bring it to you and release it. This is a skill he can benefit from throughout his lifetime for both exercise and good behavior if you shape it now.

But if you're not mindful of your eventual goal, you might default to "normal" human behavior and reprimand your puppy if he tries to pick up a forbidden object such as your sunglasses. And if he already has possession of them, most people will grab them away and scold. The lesson you *think* you are teaching is:

Fetch is a great way for children and puppies to play together.

don't pick up and chew my sunglasses. The lesson you are *actually* teaching is: when you get something good, you should run away with it because I'm going to snatch it away. Worse yet, your puppy may grow up thinking you don't want him to pick up *anything*.

There is a way you can have your cake and eat it too. You can teach your pup that some objects are more rewarding to pick up than others, but that it's always a good idea to give them to you on request. Attach a light leash of 10 to 15 feet to the pup's collar. Put that on whenever you are playing with and observing him. A young puppy should not be loose unobserved anyway, and definitely not while dragging his long leash. But when the leash is employed, rather than scolding or nagging when your puppy is headed for trouble, you can step on the line, fish a treat out of your pocket, kneel down and encourage him to come back to you. However, if you turn your head for a moment and pup already has those sunglasses, step on the line, walk calmly back to your dog, gently remove them from his mouth without any negativity, and give him an acceptable toy to hold instead. In time, he'll learn to distinguish between

Using a drag line, you can guide a puppy back to you for a reward.

Once the puppy picks up the toy, kneel down and encourage her back to you.

approved and unapproved objects without being put off the game. There will be plenty of organic moments that just arise by chance, and you can use those as teachable moments to teach fetch to a puppy.

Sometimes you'll also want to play with your puppy, and these are good opportunities to introduce short formal retrieving sessions. Start with a toy that is small and light enough for a pup to easily pick it up but large enough that he can't swallow it. Get his attention with the toy by squeaking or shaking it, then toss it a short distance away so that he can go to it, the long leash trailing behind him. When pup picks up the toy, kneel down to his level—which makes you look very inviting—and begin clapping lightly as you call him back to you in a happy voice. If he doesn't come, put a little bit of pressure on the long leash to encourage him back to you and praise as he comes toward you.

This last part of the sequence is very important. When your puppy gets to you with the toy, don't reach for it right away. Pet your puppy for a moment so that he knows you're happy but step on the line so he can't run away with the toy. Pet your way to his head and mouth and then smoothly remove the toy, giving him a treat the instant he releases the toy. If he clamps down on it, put the treat to his nose so he immediately understands the value of releasing. We call that trading, but you won't have to do it for long. He'll quickly understand the game itself is the reward. Best of all, as he grows up, you can begin to play outside and throw longer distances, which allows you to easily exercise your dog in a productive way. A tired puppy is a good puppy!

Puppies, like toddlers, often have minds of their own!

Touching Your Pup's Paws, Ears, and Mouth

Not all games have to be played with verve and enthusiasm. Some are more valuable when conducted in a calm, focused way with the puppy so he learns to enjoy or at least tolerate being held and touched in ways that will soon become important. The benefits are huge. We cannot tell you how many owners complain to us that they cannot trim their dog's nails or even touch their feet to wipe them. That is why it is so helpful to start when your puppy is young. Now is the easiest time to accustom him to having his paws touched and nails clipped. Here's how to start:

- Pick the puppy up and using your nondominant hand and arm, use what we call the football hold. Your hand will support the chest, the puppy's body nestled between your forearm and your chest. Your hand will lace between his forelegs to cradle his chest with the palm of your hand. Hold him just tight enough so that he can't wriggle free, but not so tight that he feels squished. Keep your other hand away from the puppy so he doesn't start to nibble it.

- The puppy will likely struggle to get free. Hold your ground until your puppy relaxes and accepts a moment of kindly restraint. You'll probably feel your puppy sigh or take a deep breath at that moment when he decides

to relax and accept. That is the precise moment to quietly praise and put your puppy down to play. We are teaching two crucial lessons here with this simple little game. First, we reward calm, not struggle. This helps your puppy learn to self-calm, which we call an off switch. We talked a lot more about that in Chapter 8 (page 135). And second, pup will learn to trust you and when he gets older, you'll be able to easily clean his ears and clip his nails.

- Once your puppy has learned to relax while you hold him this way, we'll add a series of new steps, one at a time.

- Use your free hand to touch the back of his head, the middle of his back, and his rear near the hips. Pause and keep your fingers still in each location for 2 or 3 seconds.

- Touch the top of a front leg lightly, then proceed down the leg, quietly praising, ending at the paw. Work at this periodically until you can touch all four legs with a relatively calm puppy. Your puppy will get used to having his paws touched and associating this positively. You can also lightly squeeze between the toes with praise. Once the pup is not reacting in any negative fashion to this, you are ready for nail trimming. At this age, just the little hook at the very tips of the nails can then be clipped once a week and this will set an important precedent. Start with one nail per session.

- Conclude the session with an upbeat period of fun on the floor or ground, using a preferred toy.

Come When Called Games

As we said earlier when discussing fetch games, be mindful that coming when called should *always* feel like a rewarding game for puppies. It might not seem obvious at first, but behaviors are connected like puzzle pieces. If we scold for picking up wrong household objects after calling the puppy to us so we can take them away, we are not teaching the lesson we intend. What the puppy may be learning from his first days in your home is that obeying isn't always a good idea. Fetch is coming when called in order to bring us back a toy we threw. Coming when called is moving directly to you simply because you asked. Eventually this game will become a life safety insurance policy. We can teach the puppy to leave that electrical cord alone and run to us for praise and treats instead. We can start it now, teaching a series of simple activities that your puppy will find rewarding.

- We'll use food to start. The best treat is small enough that your puppy can eat it in a single gulp. Use a moist, healthy treat. If your treats are too big or too chewy, cut them in smaller pieces.

- Begin by luring the pup into following you. Place a treat right at your puppy's nose, almost touching it. Keep the treat there and walk backward as he follows. Vary the distances you go, but always try to move at least a few feet so pup understands that coming when called involves distance. Let him eat it once you stop and he's close and in front of you.

- As the puppy starts looking forward to the game, you can add a sit once he gets to you and you've stopped. As you stop walking backward, raise the treat only slightly above the puppy's nose, drawing his attention upward. Then move it an inch or two toward his forehead. He'll realize that he can easily take the treat if he sits. Let him eat it the instant he sits.

- You can now extend the distance to 15 or 20 feet holding a light dragline in case your puppy says he's too busy to come when you call. Crouch down and

Kneeling and holding out a toy or treat will encourage puppies to quickly learn recall.

open your arms as an invitation or clap lightly for attention as you call. Always praise. But at this stage, use a treat reward only every second or third time.

- If your puppy doesn't come when you call as above, don't reprimand, but use the line to help him to you. Let him sniff the treat he would have gotten had he listened the first time, but don't give it to him. However, give him a second chance a few seconds later. Give him two or three treats this time to make your point.

- Once pup has the idea, you can now turn the exercise into a game of "come and find me." Hide around a corner or a piece of furniture and call. When he finds you, give him a treat or favorite toy. As he learns the nature of the game, you can extend the distance of where you go to hide, and he'll have fun finding you. He won't even realize he's learning the *come* command.

- When you are outside in the backyard, you can extend this game to hiding behind trees or rows of bushes.

Self-Confidence Exercises

At New Skete and at Marc's Little Dog Farm, we use children's jungle gyms and ramps to accustom pups to getting up onto a platform. It's not only fun for them to play on, but also especially handy for such future tasks as grooming and nail trimming plus it builds confidence. It can also be easily turned into a game that the puppy enjoys. The options will grow as the puppy begins to get older, and you can easily use crates and pieces of agility equipment such as tunnels and ramps to keep things interesting and fun for your pup. We covered agility for older dogs in Chapter 7 (page 119), but there are benefits to getting your puppy started early.

- Make a low bridge by using two cinder blocks, or anything stable and not too tall, and connect them with a wide board that is only a few feet long. Help the puppy onto one side of the bridge, support him so he doesn't fall, and gently encourage him forward along the plank. Don't force him, but you can use a treat to lure him forward. You will quickly wean out the treat as he learns. Praise warmly as he goes forward.

Supervised puppy play builds confidence at the Monks of New Skete and Marc's Chicago area farm.

- Another step in this process is creating a stable and gently sloped ramp on both sides of the bridge so you can guide your puppy up, across, and down. By guiding the pup up the ascent, across the bridge, and then down the ascent, you will see her self-confidence building and how you can easily craft this into a game that she delights in.

- Once your puppy is confident on a wide bridge, he'll be equally at ease on a low platform or table, but be sure it has a nonskid surface. This will become a perfect place to practice brushing and nail clipping. Elevating the puppy slightly encourages him to hold still and you won't break your back bending over so much.

- Agility tunnels can be lots of fun and build confidence for a pup who has learned to scamper through them. One person helps the puppy into the tunnel, wearing a long leash that has been fed through to the other side. To start, be sure the tunnel is straight rather than curved, so your puppy can see you when you crouch down at the other end and encourage him through.

Quiet Time: The Value of a Good Bone

We usually associate games with heightened activities that wear our puppy out. But it is helpful to remember that purposeful play totally engages the dog in something enjoyable while it also curbs some impulses such as biting. Instead, it favors better decisions, such as cooperation. When looked at from this perspective, our understanding of games can expand to include calming activities that occupy the dog's attention for substantial periods of time.

- With the pup on a leash to help keep him near you, guide him into a down next to you. And give him a bone or chew that he really likes. You can spread a tiny bit of peanut butter on it to get the puppy interested quickly. Quietly praise while he is chewing.

- Once or twice, interrupt her chewing by taking the bone as you say *leave it*, and immediately offer a treat. You are trading things of value. Praise warmly, then give her the bone back to chew. This game will help prevent possessiveness at the same time as it allows your pup to be with you calmly instead of demanding attention.

- If your puppy growls at you during this exercise, try using a lower-value item like a plain nylon bone that the pup won't be as possessive with. Continue following the above advice, using a treat when you take the nylon bone.

The Potty Game for Housebreaking

Housebreaking is very simple for some puppies (or older dogs) but can get complicated with others. It's the luck of the draw whether you have a pup who seems to just "get it" in the first weeks, or if your puppy doesn't understand that there are places he should eliminate, and places where he should not. That's why we have devised a housebreaking game to add a bit of lighthearted enjoyment into what can otherwise seem like drudgery. There are numerous benefits to this game. Among them are these:

- You will learn a great deal about how the puppy's biology and psychology come together in elimination behavior.

- Although you can't count on children to do all the work for you, the Potty Game will help engage them in a family-wide effort.

- Once the puppy begins to understand the game, you can teach him to ring a bell, signaling that he has to go outside for those dogs who are being trained for outdoor potty. You'll find that game next.

- This game works for puppies learning to use outdoor potty and those who are learning to use pads.

- We'll talk mostly about outdoor elimination because that is what we usually recommend. But for pad training, if you must, you'll take your puppy to a pad or a puppy pen containing his pads at the appropriate moments.

We need to get a few preliminaries out of the way so the game will be as easy as possible for both you and the pup.

- What goes in must come out. Avoid foods with any of these ingredients: wheat, corn, soy, byproducts. Although this is not a complete list, these are among the most common culprits in foods that contain a lot of fillers, and therefore, produce frequent and large stools. Dogs also seem to need more water when fed these foods. All this can make potty training more difficult, especially in complicated cases.

- In our experience, grain-free kibbles also produce more stool. Discuss with your veterinarian or research online veterinary nutrition resources for more information.

- It is *imperative* that you feed on a regular schedule. If you are not feeding at the same times every day, the puppy's schedule will be random and difficult to manage.

- Crate training will be *very* useful when playing this game because there are moments you'll need to confine your puppy when you cannot carefully observe him. We wrote extensively about crate training "how-tos" in *Let Dogs Be Dogs*, our dog psychology book. And a bit later in this chapter we'll give you a game called Follow the Treat . . . into Your Crate to make this part even easier for you and your puppy. Crate your puppy when you cannot observe him.

- Although we don't recommend you restrict water for your puppy, it is important to know when he has imbibed a lot of it. Keep an eye on him and if he drinks a lot of water at once, understand he will need to go out soon after drinking, and then up to twice more at relatively quick intervals. If he has overhydrated, it won't all come out at once. It will take a few trips outside, spaced a bit apart.

- You will find this game *much* easier to play once you have a sense of your puppy's natural elimination schedule. To get a good sense of that and to play the game, start writing down the times of his meals, water intake, and successful outdoor episodes categorized by liquid and solid. Do the same for any accidents. Keep this written potty diary on a clipboard that you can place on the puppy's crate for easy access.

- Don't let your puppy out into the yard alone. Go with him. Stay with him and observe carefully, so you know exactly what he has done. Remember, you'll need to come inside and record that right away.

HOW TO PLAY

Your goal is to accumulate 30 points. Once you, your family, and the puppy have reached 30 points as a team, your puppy is either potty trained, or, if he's much under 20 weeks, he has become predictable and a great deal more reliable. While this doesn't mean you can stop paying attention to the schedule and your pup's needs, it does mean the job is far, far easier with few, if any, mistakes.

HOW DO YOU WIN POINTS?

It's easy! You get one point for every 24 hours that your puppy does not have an accident. And since you only need 30 points, it should be simple, right? Well, yes, if you do everything right it is . . . but there's a catch:

Deduct 3 points for any accident! And that is really the wildcard in the Potty Game.

When you start, let's say you have 3 successful days in a row. Now you have three points! But then on the fourth day, maybe your feeding schedule got off kilter, perhaps you weren't quite as vigilant, and you didn't notice that the puppy had guzzled more water than usual. Puppy had a pee accident in the kitchen on the morning of the 4th day, and a poop accident in his crate that afternoon. Now we have to deduct six points from the three we had already accumulated. That means that as the fourth day draws to a close, our score is *negative* three. Sadly, we will spend the next three days starting over and getting back to zero so we can begin to make progress.

You might ask, why such a heavy deduction? Potty training is all about building patterns so that the puppy actually *wants* to get to his special spot, be that his pad or outdoors where you will take him. At first, our job is to *anticipate* when the puppy will need to eliminate. We can do that better by filling out the potty diary we mentioned. But eventually, especially as he gets a bit older, we'll be asking the puppy to tolerate a bit of discomfort until we get him outside. In the next game, we'll help you and your puppy learn a signaling system, but we still must understand that potty training is very much about patterns of behavior—what the puppy is thoroughly used to doing, he will eventually *want* to do. And if that happens to be the *wrong* thing, we need time and multiple successes to rebuild and strengthen the pattern we actually want.

- If you have children and want to involve them, that's fine. Even young children can participate, but we must stress parental oversight and involvement for safety and progress.

- It is very important for you to keep accurate records so you can keep score. Filling out a daily potty diary will not only help you keep score but will also help you uncover any weak spots in your schedule. We can't stress that enough.

- It truly helps to view this as more of a game than a chore. For children, or even for your own amusement, start a calendar on day 1. Hang the calendar in the kitchen and celebrate successful days by placing a happy face sticker on a day where you and the puppy score a point. Place one sad face sticker for each accident that day. If you're diligent, you'll see a lot more happy faces than sad.

Once you get to 30 points, the hardest part is over. You have established both a schedule and an understanding of housebreaking between you and your dog. Congratulations! Remain mindful of how you got there so you can continue to strengthen this good pattern of behavior.

Ring the Potty Bell

Wouldn't it be great if you could teach your puppy to ring a bell whenever he has to go out to potty? Thousands of owners have asked us about this trick, and it is not difficult to teach if you know the steps and are consistent with your pup. Although there are a lot of steps, they are easy, and you will see the logic in them as you progress.

First, a couple of preliminaries. Your puppy must be housetrained for the potty bell to be useful. If the puppy is already trained to eliminate outside, you'll have a much easier time of associating the bell with getting out to his designated spot. If you need help with potty training, definitely start the Potty Game first.

Hang jingle bells, or bells made for puppies, from the specific door you will use to take him out. Place them at the puppy's nose level. If you don't have a fenced yard for training purposes only, first attach a leash to the puppy's collar so that once he rings the bell, you can take him out *instantly* and not lose time fiddling with a leash.

Now you're ready to begin.

- Pick a time when you suspect he will have to go, but not a moment that is terribly urgent. Hold the leash a couple of feet from your dog. Let him watch you smear a tiny little bit of peanut butter on the dangling bell. Do not hold him back or away from the bell as you do this. Never reprimand for curiosity regarding the bell. Naturally, he'll want to lick at the bell. He's a puppy and it smells and tastes of peanut butter! As he sniffs and licks at the bell, it will make a sound.

- When he has licked the peanut butter off the bell, calmly and quietly open the door. Walk him to your preferred spot. Do not talk to him unless it is to follow the Potty on Command directions in Chapter 6 (page 102). Allow him to sniff and potty, and once he empties himself, praise softly with a quiet word. No need to give a food treat because eliminating feels good to the puppy. It relieves pressure.

- Once back in the house you can turn your dog loose under observation. If she ignores the bell, don't worry about it. She may know there's no peanut butter left. But if she starts sniffing and licking at the bell, let her do so without interruption. After a little ringing, simply take the leash, open the door, and let her out again. She probably won't need to go. Simply give her a quiet moment outdoors. Then, with no praise, no touch, and no treat, bring her back into the house.

- If he immediately becomes obsessive about the bell, gate him out of the room only if he has eliminated and you know him to be completely empty. Or you can briefly remove the bell because you know he won't need it for a while.

- Since you know his potty schedule, for the next 3 days, each time you believe your dog has to go, leash him, rub a bit of treat on the bell and go through the bell and potty sequence. Most puppies quickly grasp the concept. After the third day, begin to make the peanut butter appear on the bell sometimes, but not others, perhaps every other time. Do this for a week. This makes the treat component of the exercise random, and studies have shown that random, intermittent reinforcement is a very powerful form of reward. During this week let her out whenever she rings the bell, whether the treat was there or not.

- After the first week, clever dogs will experiment by ringing the bell to go outside when they want to play. We call this a false alarm. Give your dog 3 or 4 minutes, outside but if you realize she just wanted to play, quietly, without a word, bring her back inside and crate her for 20 minutes.

- It's important not to give negative energy to your dog or to become impatient and pressure her. Simply show her that she earns a brief but noticeable timeout with a false alarm. She'll figure it out quickly. After all, she was clever enough to conceive of the tactic in the first place.

Voilà, now you have a dog who is ringing a bell to go outside and potty!

Follow the Treat . . . into Your Crate Game

Most owners who adopt a puppy will want to housetrain him as one of the very first tasks on their "to do" list. Crates are invaluable tools for this process. The Monks wrote about them in *The Art of Raising a Puppy* and together we provided a lot of crate information in *Let Dogs Be Dogs*. We'll talk about it here as we did in Chapter 5 (page 87), presenting the crate as a game so it can remain a happy constant through-out your dog's life. When you housetrain a puppy properly, he learns to view the crate as a safe "den" where he can rest and eat his meals. You can easily build on this foundation by making a game out of going into the crate. If he looks forward to being there, you've already won half the battle. Here's how to play the game:

- When the puppy is not looking, place a trail of high-value treats (cheese bits or small pieces of freeze-dried liver, for example) leading up to and into the crate. Place the treats close enough to each other so your puppy can easily follow them. Leave the crate door open. Guide him to the beginning of the trail facing toward the crate. When you let go of her, say, *crate, go to your house,* or any cute command you'll consistently use. As he starts following the trail, praise him quietly. When he goes into the crate, close the door, and drop a few more treats inside. You can open it once he has eaten them. But he'll quickly learn that closing the door is a good thing.

- Later, as you repeat the process, lengthen the distance between treats. Make it more interesting by closing the crate door with a jackpot of extra treats just inside the door so that when the pup gets to the crate she'll start to paw at the door, trying to get in. Don't make her wait too long, but her desire to get inside will be a powerful learning tool. In this case, delayed gratification is your friend.

Puppies are naturally playful. It's part of their makeup. Good puppy activities, play with a purpose, offers you immeasurable opportunity to not only bond with your puppy, but also to teach good behavior beginning at the very start of the relationship. You can set the stage now for good behavior later. That's because your little friend is a sponge for information. Because she is new to the world, your puppy is absorbing an incredible array of facts and assumptions not just daily, but *constantly*.

For example, don't call your puppy and then scold her. She might draw the conclusion that coming when called is not always a good idea. Unintended consequences can quickly complicate your relationship.

That's why we have given you lots of productive activities in this chapter. We want both *you* and your puppy to learn good behavior as you play. Finally, enjoy every moment. Because there is some work to raising a puppy, time may seem to drag at first. But puppyhood lasts for only the briefest flash of time. Enjoy it. And take lots of pictures!

CHAPTER 10

Socializing Dogs So They Can Play Together

So far, we have spent a good deal of time speaking about how owners can play with their dogs in a way that enhances their relationship. We've suggested many games and strategies to teach your dog better behavior as you play. But this is only part of the equation. An equally important dimension of dog play goes right back to his earliest days in the litter, playing safely with other dogs. A well-adjusted dog can learn how to play with other dogs appropriately and in a way that expends energy as he's having fun. This is essential for a dog's overall well-being, yet often it doesn't just happen naturally. Sure, there are some dogs who learn to interact with other dogs almost effortlessly, but most trainers would agree this is more the exception than the rule. It is significant that a common question dog owners ask us is: "How do I get my dog to play nicely with other dogs?" No doubt indicating that they've had some rough moments in this regard.

We recall a stressed owner asking for advice on how to help his Siberian husky get along with other dogs. "I got him as a rescue because I was working at home and felt I could take care of him, but I didn't really have the chance to socialize him all that much. I exercised him primarily in my backyard. He's good at fetch and it was a great way of burning off energy. But when I relocated to the city, I noticed him being both fearful and even reactive to the dogs we came upon. It was so embarrassing. The more I tried to avoid other dogs, the worse his behavior got. I'm desperate. What can I do?" We assured the gentleman that his case wasn't hopeless, but that the solution was going to involve training and desensitizing. While it is understandable why

his dog wasn't properly socialized, the consequences of this were going to demand much more time and effort to fix than would ordinarily be the case.

Being some of nature's most sociable creatures, there's little doubt that dogs love to play with other dogs— at least some of the time, and many owners understandably would love to see their dogs enjoy themselves by romping around with other dogs. But there is plenty of evidence to suggest that unless play is introduced wisely, it can turn into something dangerous. The casebooks of trainers who have worked with clients whose dogs are aggressive with other dogs are legion, reflecting the fact that many owners simply don't know how to safely familiarize their dogs with other dogs. A sensible start is the foundation that allows dogs to play safely. In this chapter we will discuss the many aspects of socializing dogs so that they can play. We'll consider how best to introduce your dog to another dog, how to introduce a new dog you've adopted to a dog you already have, and how to create appropriate play between your own dogs. In addition, we'll look at how to interpret different styles of canine play along with play behaviors that can cause trouble. Finally, we'll look at popular options such as doggy day care and dog parks that provide you and your dog with opportunities for additional play.

Introducing Your Dog to Another Dog

Many owners expect that their dog will instantly make friends with every dog they meet whether on a leash walk or loose at a dog park. All too often though, thrusting dogs together without understanding how to best help them make the introduction can unwittingly trigger an aggressive encounter. Although some dogs are not put off by a strange dog moving right into their face, immediately going nose-to-nose, many will object to what is considered rude among dogs.

Imagine that you are walking down a street, minding your own business, when a large fellow—a complete stranger—steps into your path, blocking your forward movement. In less than a second, he's hugging you and ruffling your hair. That encounter is not likely to go well. You'll feel assaulted and you will respond in any one of a number of ways, none of them good.

On the other hand, if the same fellow pauses at an appropriate social distance and says, "Excuse me, I just moved into the neighborhood and I see you have a dog. By any chance can you tell me where the nearest dog friendly park is?"

You are likely to have a much better response, and you'll point to where the park is located. Or you might even be going in that direction yourself and so you invite him to walk his dog parallel to you and yours. This could function as a manageable icebreaker that allows the dogs to get used to each other as they walk along. The man then says, "Thanks so much. My name is Joe, and this is my dog, Molly." You respond by introducing yourself and your dog and you both continue on your way toward the park. As you walk along you observe that the dogs seem comfortable in each other's presence, both walking nicely and in control. When you reach the park, you explain to Joe that you have an appointment and so won't be using the park today but that perhaps you'll see him and Molly in the future. A few days later, entering the park with your dog, you spot Joe playing with Molly. When Molly sees your dog, she starts wagging her tail happily. As you turn your dog loose to play, Joe also waves, so you walk over to chat. Meanwhile, the two dogs start to romp together nearby.

This is the way people meet, become acquainted and then perhaps eventually pursue a friendship. And it's similar for dogs—in their own way of course. When two dogs are leashed, it is difficult for them to introduce themselves to one another politely, in the way dogs usually will if left to their own devices. Given the option, they will rarely go nose-to-nose immediately, as this is generally considered rude. Depending on the dog, it can also *be* or at least *be perceived* as a challenge.

If loose in an open space, they are far more likely to circle one another for a

moment to make the initial introductions by sniffing in those doglike areas that embarrass people, but which is a polite form of inquiry and greeting among dogs.

Allowing, or even encouraging, dogs to meet face to face, even if you've repeatedly gotten away with it, just isn't a good idea. That's because the dogs have no chance to adjust to each other, and often the rigid body language can provoke drama. We have seen this happen in any variety of settings and it never fails to make us cringe. However, there can be times when you might let your dog meet another when the other dog's body language makes it evident that it can be done safely. If you do choose to let your dog meet another while it is on leash, be sure not to have them meet nose to nose. Instead, walk them slightly past each other so that each dog has the chance to sniff the other dog's flank. Always be on the lookout for any signs of stiffening, raised hackles, or low growling. If you see any of these signs, end the meeting and move on.

People often ask us what to do when other people ask, "Can my dog say hello to your dog?" Assuming that you would prefer not to, here's what we would do: we know full well this is not the place to take off the leashes so the dogs can make dog-appropriate introductions. So, at the risk of seeming aloof, we smile, continue walking without breaking pace, and reply, "I'm sorry, we're training right now but see you at the dog park."

You don't need to feel guilty about not wanting your dog to stop and meet every dog it comes upon during a walk. While it is healthy for him to socialize with other dogs, that is best organized between dogs he'll meet again and again, like those belonging to family and friends. Or in a setting where the introductions can be off leash (for more natural dog behavior) and curated by people who know what they're looking at to prevent trouble before it occurs.

Progressive, structured introductions are always better than playing Russian roulette. Here's how you can help your dog make friends with a dog he can see again, such as one owned by a friend, neighbor, or family member:

- Ask a friend with a stable dog if she'd be willing to take a walk with you and your dog. Meet in neutral territory that neither of the dogs claims as his own turf. Both dogs should be on leash, but don't let them interact at the beginning. Instead, go for a purposeful walk with the dogs, keeping them a few feet apart from each other.

- Keep moving forward side by side with your friend, with at least one of you between the dogs. This allows the dogs to gradually adjust to the presence of one other as they go. Walking in a neutral area will keep the dogs interested in the environment instead of focusing only on each other.

- At first the dogs will likely exhibit a bit of excitement, but as you continue to walk, taking pressure off them, you'll notice increasingly relaxed body language. There will be less staring. Jumpiness or tension will decrease as they focus less on each other and more on the shared experience. Dogs who first signaled intensity with closed mouths and tails held high will unstiffen, lowering the tails to a more casual position, opening the mouths to breathe more naturally, sometimes with a dog "smile." These are some of the signs that signal their growing comfort with the other dog in proximity. Don't be discouraged if it takes several walks before the dogs seem used to one another. It just depends on the individuals and the comfort level they experience with each other.

- Whether after a single walk, or several over the course of days, as you sense the dogs becoming relaxed, it's time for the next step, allowing them to move more freely together. Use an open area such as a backyard or field with the dogs on long lines where they can run around when you eventually drop the line. This is far preferable to going directly into a closed space such as your house to introduce them formally. Having them on a line or a leash enables the dogs to move around and evaluate each other's body language while also giving you the opportunity to pick up the leashes and easily move them apart should things start getting out of hand. Note: never leave training collars, such as prong collars, on dogs when they're playing because they can easily tangle in another dog's equipment. That can cause a fight.

- At this point you can allow them to greet each other, with each handler holding the leash loose, allowing them to sniff each other's butts but preventing them from meeting nose-to-nose quite yet. *Avoid tensing up and tightening the leashes.* You may have to move as the dogs circle one another so they do not tangle. After a few moments, you can move the dogs apart, take a brief break then allow them to return to each other.

- It's always a good idea to break the play up in short segments in the beginning as this keeps them from getting too excited. As they become used to each other you can lengthen the play sessions with less concern that things will get out of hand.

- If all goes well, you can drop the leashes on this encounter, or after a walk on the next one. Dog play often gets pretty wild at first and can even look like mock combat. If both dogs seem to be enjoying themselves, you can let it go. But if one dog seems to feel overwhelmed or tries to stop but the other won't let him, pick up both leashes and separate the dogs for a breather.

- Most dogs will do well if you follow these protocols at first. Do watch to make sure one dog is not overwhelming the other. If he is, then call him off to interrupt the overly boisterous play so his new buddy will still enjoy him. But well-matched dogs with similar play styles will happily exhaust one another. You'll appreciate that when you go home, and your dog quickly lies down to sleep it off for a few hours.

Giving Your Dog a Playmate

If life with one dog is great, how much better would it be to have another? You'll have double the fun and your first dog will always have someone to play with. Dogs that live with each other can more easily engage in play when the spirit moves them, and there are clear behavioral advantages to this. Well, that can be the case, assuming you understand that having two dogs requires much more work and if you have a clear idea of how to bring a new dog into the household. We will focus on helping you create a good relationship between your old friend and a new one.

But before we jump into the how-to, here are two points to consider. First, is your current dog healthy enough to enjoy company? There is no cutoff age to enjoy having a buddy. But do think about his age and especially his physical condition. If your dog is 13 and frail, think twice about adding a young boisterous dog into the mix at this time. Second, have you spent years doting on your dog? Would you smile and admit he's at least a bit spoiled? As you start thinking about bringing in a new dog, remember it means your current dog will have to share you and everything in his home, and that may come as a bit of a surprise to him. You can prepare for it by training a bit more and spoiling a bit less in the weeks prior to adopting. We have written entire books if you want to know a lot more about those topics. *The Art of Training Your Dog* shows you how to train, and *Let Dogs Be Dogs* discusses how to understand dog psychology so multiple dogs (and you) can live happily together.

Let's assume you have thought it through, and you have decided it's a great time to add another dog to the pack. Here's how to do it safely:

- Start with the guidelines above as when introducing a new dog. Have a friend or family member hold the new dog's leash somewhere off your property. You'll arrive at the rendezvous location with your dog also on leash. Then go for the same walk we described earlier in which the dogs are essentially asked to ignore one another. Keep them moving forward in a steady manner. Go for a long walk and as you go, the dogs will be getting used to the presence of one another in an organized, low-pressure way.

- Assuming that the dogs seem to be fairly relaxed, allow them to briefly interact in an open area. That might be your yard or an open field near your home. Keep them on leashes as above and keep the initial interactions short. The handlers can gently use the leashes to pull the dogs apart, move away a little to relieve any tension, and then come back together. If the response is positive, you can allow them to sniff each other's butts and mid sections. Avoid walking them right into each other's faces where they will have no choice but to go nose to nose. Their body language will dictate how to proceed, but hopefully the steady progression of exposure will lead to a playful and relaxed interaction. Now it's time to bring them into the home.

- When you reach your home, let the new dog go in first with you to have the opportunity to sniff around and get adjusted while on leash. You don't want the dog who has been living with you to put pressure on the new dog, so it's best to keep him outside for a time. Then when you bring in your existing dog, also on leash, keep the preliminary interactions brief and positive. Afterward, you may choose to use dog gates or crates to keep the dogs separate for a time to allow them to relax and adjust in each other's presence.

- It's important for the first few days to keep the interactions with each other short and controlled. Feed the dogs separately, and if possible, with your helper, walk them together through the neighborhood as before. Mutual walks help solidify that they are becoming a team, packmates. Following this sequence faithfully will help the dogs adjust to each other quickly and begin to really enjoy each other's presence.

- A final word. For the first couple of weeks, it is a good idea to allow the new dog to wear a leash attached to his collar under observation. You can easily pick it up if you need to move him away from something, including your other dog. If you have high-value chew toys laying around the house, now is the time to pick them all up and put them away. You no longer own just one dog; you have two, and we must help them avoid competing for resources such as rawhide, bully sticks, and bones. You can give those to the dogs when at least one of them is crated.

While you should oversee interactions, your older dog can help you show a puppy how to behave.

Encouraging Appropriate Play between Your Own Dogs

When two dogs live together, it is important to foster positive play and to disallow the type of play that can lead to conflicts between them. The age and temperaments of the dogs will affect the type of play that is best for them. For example, it is not uncommon for owners with an aging dog to obtain a puppy because they know the older dog will not be with them forever. A second dog provides comfort and also creates the opportunity for the older dog to teach the younger dog the ropes. This is fine, and many owners have had outstanding results by working the younger dog into the household in this way. But we need to stress several cautions. Often an older dog will not want to play as frequently as the younger, and owners should be alert to that. If the younger dog keeps demanding to play with the older dog, pestering and mouthing him, the older dog can get cranky and lash out. Recognize this in advance and end any play session your older dog is truly resisting. He may have arthritis and find it painful unless he has enough quiet time to recover. Always end on a good note, and pay a bit of special attention to your original pal.

It's also a good idea to match the dogs' temperaments. If your first dog is mild mannered around other dogs, she might feel bullied by a rowdy newcomer with a "frat boy" personality. This doesn't mean they can't get along and actually learn to enjoy one another. But it does mean you should be observant so you can interrupt

Brother Christopher spends time with his original pal.

any play that is overwhelming a dog. Signs that a dog feels overwhelmed include repeated attempts to withdraw from play, trying to leave the area to stop the engagement, and constantly turning her back on the other dog. In the more extreme cases, a dog may cower or snarl and growl in an attempt to stop the other dog from engaging too often or too hard. Keep an eye on this and separate the dogs *before* these signs are apparent. Instead, take action the moment you can predict they're about to occur if the new kid doesn't back off. Keep play sessions between the dogs appropriate to their age and temperament. Periodically crating the new dog will give your older dog both a mental and physical break.

Some dogs don't care much about toys. Others may fiercely love a special toy above all others. If both dogs fixate on the same toy, it can lead to possessive- ness and drama. Avoid play sessions where the dogs are competing for a preferred object. It is much safer to let the dogs play together, rough housing and chasing after each other around the yard or gently wrestling in the house, without the pres- ence of toys to compete for. Remove toys that are likely to create conflict and give access to them when the dogs are tired and while you can observe. In some cases, it's better to just remove them altogether. Sometimes sacrifices must be made for the greater good!

Interpreting Different Styles of Canine Play

There is no question that not all dogs play alike. They have unique play styles that are influenced by breed, upbringing, and their own personalities. It is helpful to be aware of this and to understand your dog's play style so you can match it with his new friend. For example, the New Skete German shepherds love rough play with each other—wrestling and even body-slamming with bared teeth—and it is not uncommon for a visitor to misinterpret what we know to be good-natured fun as aggressive behavior. Our shepherds love to ritually "spar" with each other martial arts style. In fact, all dogs do this. You'll often see it in the dog park or play groups. It can get out of hand if we are not watchful. If we sense that the play is excessively intensifying, we break it up before it escalates. For the most part dogs are respon-

The message is, "Hey, want to play?"

But it is this crouching play bow that actually starts the game.

When dogs stand face to face, it often means we're about to play . . . or fight. The relaxed facial expressions and postures tell you this encounter is playful.

When one dog has had enough, a polite playmate will stop and permit him to rest.

sive to our guidance and learn restraint through such playful interactions. Trust us, there is a world of difference between two dogs "mock-fighting" and a bona fide dog fight. The latter is primal and can lead to serious injury.

So, what other styles of canine play might there be?

- Well, if you have a herding or hound breed in particular, you may see your dog come alive in chasing games. But dogs of all breeds sometimes enjoy the thrill of the chase. Often these dogs will spontaneously erupt in a game of Tag, You're It. It's a riot watching them take turns being both chaser and target, alternating positions, and racing around a yard. Their facial expressions reflect the joy of companionship and exercise. It is amazing how long some dogs can continue to run. Talk about Olympic marathoners! They also do well with games such as frisbee and flyball.

- Other dogs will participate in play more indirectly—let's call this the "sports fan" style, excitedly watching a group of dogs play while they stay on the sidelines, running back and forth to track the activity. They prefer being on the periphery rather than right in the middle of the play. Sometimes they sit to observe.

- Then we have dogs who love tugging and keep away. One dog will find a stick or a toy and tease another with it, as if to say "Look what I have! You don't have one!" Before long, the dogs are happily playing tug, one on either side. This is fine so long as it doesn't devolve into possessive behavior. As an owner, it is important to know your dog and whether such tugging has led to unwanted possessiveness. But tug often turns into chasing behavior that can occupy the dogs for an entire play session.

- Finally, there are those dogs who are content to keep themselves occupied by themselves with a toy and really don't require another dog to interact with. They are more the "lone wolf" type, and they can be seen tossing a ball to themselves and pouncing or even running around the yard chasing birds and insects. There is nothing wrong with a dog who is content with his own company.

Play Behaviors That Can Cause Trouble

As dogs interact and play with each other, things can get out of hand if no one is watching for signs of trouble brewing. It is important for owners to be aware of these sparks before they flame up into something serious. The Monks and Marc receive dozens of calls every year after a scuffle or even a real fight, problems that could easily have been prevented. Prevention is the best cure when it comes to dog play gone wrong.

Watch out for the following behaviors and interrupt them:

Mounting, aka humping. You'll see this behavior from time to time in a dog park. While the usual culprit is male, certain females will also mount other dogs. Either way, the behavior does not always indicate sexual attraction. Quite often it expresses a display of dominance over the other dog. Some dogs are fairly tolerant of being restrained in this way. But others will respond aggressively to what they perceive as a challenge. They will whip around to discipline the guilty party. Before you know it, you can have a full-blown fight on your hands. It is important for owners to interrupt this behavior when they see it developing. A dog about to mount will position himself behind the other dog, laying his head on the back of the other. The owner should immediately call their dog and approach quickly even before it begins. Sometimes this will be enough to prevent a recurrence. If your dog is a repeat offender, do not turn him loose with multiple dogs until you have dealt with the problem on a training level. If your dog is the "victim," remove him from the situation so he doesn't have to aggress in order to defend himself.

Top: *Although it doesn't always, humping can definitely cause a dog fight.*

Bottom: *Laying the head over another dog's neck can be perceived as pushy or domineering by the first dog.*

Neck biting. Watch out for this behavior when dogs run together or play chase. Although any dog may do it, neck biting during play is especially prevalent among hunting and herding breeds. We believe it is a vestigial instinct to take down prey. During the chase, one dog starts to nip at the neck of the other. But this can provoke a retaliatory response from the first dog. If you see this, go back to shorter play sessions with two handlers present, keeping the dogs from getting too worked up all at once. Playing in a smaller area often lowers the excitement level because the dogs don't have as much space to run. Since neck biting most often happens at a full run, reducing space can help. You can also call the offender back to you just as he starts the behavior. A dog will often modify his play style once he realizes you will stop him every time he makes a forbidden move.

Toy stealing. Some dogs will happily share a toy, even their favorite one. Others are possessive to varying degrees. The dog who registers serious objection to another dog trying to take his toy will immediately growl and flash teeth at the offender. Unchecked, such disputes can lead to fights over objects whether between your own dogs or at a park. Owners need to have an honest understanding of their dogs. Remove toys where you can. And where you can't, if your dog is the offender, teach him a *leave it* command so he can enjoy playing with other dogs without causing a problem. Our book, *The Art of Training Your Dog*, will help those who want to teach their dogs a *leave it* command, even from a distance. If your dog is being bullied over his own toy, temporarily remove it from the equation.

In your face. Be vigilant watching for the "in your face" dog. This is one who comes up to another head on, nose-to-nose. This is a recipe for disaster. Polite dog interactions start with nose to tail introductions. But there are two kinds of dogs who may skip the niceties and approach quickly, thrusting their face right in the face of the other dog. The first is an overly friendly dog who just doesn't know or care about the rules of proper canine etiquette. This dog is saying, "The heck with introductions. Let's play *now*!" He is wiggling and inviting play in his posture. It's rude but he means no harm. The second in-your-face dog means to challenge. He's saying, "I'm in your face. What are you going to do about it?" He is stiff and glaring. While one dog will be

tolerant of another who leaps right into his face, another will register objections. One or both dogs stiffen, and before you know it you have a fight on your hands. As we've already stressed, dogs should be trained how to meet each other politely, sniffing the rear part of the other dog and letting his own rear be sniffed. This is Canine Etiquette 101 and the dog who masters it will save his owner a lot of grief.

Doggy Day Care

From the trajectory of this chapter it should be clear we believe that meeting and interacting with other dogs in a healthy way is an important skill. It is also one we want to help you understand and learn so you can help your dog develop social skills in an intentional way instead of just winging it. That's because we want you and your dog to enjoy an enriched life together. If he can play with other dogs in a positive way, it will provide him with a level of social fulfillment. If that play is a resource you both simultaneously grant him and also use to help him learn, your role as a great owner expands exponentially. A bonus is you are likely to find your dog a more obedient pet who is easier to live with. After all, dogs are social animals, and they crave the company of their own kind.

Decades ago, as we wrote in our book *Let Dogs Be Dogs*, it was not uncommon for rural and even suburban families to open the door to let their dog hang out with the neighborhood dogs, unattended. They came back when they got hungry or when whistled home for dinner. Dog fights were extremely rare. We theorize that's because dogs taught one another how to behave. Good behavior was rewarded with more play and better relationships. Sadly, dogs sometimes got hit by cars, got lost or had unwanted litters. These days it is more the exception than the rule to let dogs run loose while unattended.

In more recent times, doggy day care facilities offer to fill the gap in a way that provides exercise and mental stimulation during the day while the owners are at work. For many who can afford it, this is a far better option than simply leaving the dog home alone during the day. One enthusiastic client reported to us, "When Aldo comes home at the end of the day, he's tuckered out, which makes him so much easier to be with. We take him for a nice evening walk and then he chills until it's time for bed." Day care prices vary depending on where you live and what sort of amenities the facility offers. Not only do prices vary, but so does the quality of care which depends on factors such as how knowledgeable the staff is and the number of dogs in a room at any one time.

In 2004, Suzanne Golter opened Happy Hound Play & Daycare, Inc., in Oakland, California. Initially she was looking for a day care for own dog. She found only one and said, "The interview with me and my dog felt very sterile, and the facility did not seem warm and inviting. I left that place, sat in my car and thought, 'I can do this better.' So, I built a better, loving, caring facility."

We like day cares that are transparent and above board about their policies. It is important that they answer your questions thoroughly, especially about how they evaluate and manage dogs. Are they watchful for play that may turn edgy and that can lead to a fight? Do they interrupt the behaviors we mentioned above, and if so, how? Do they have a live video camera feed so you can see your dog during the day? Do they have separate play groups for dogs of different sizes and play styles? These are some of the questions you'll want to ask as well as asking for references.

Owners will be asked to provide proof of vaccination for rabies, DHPP (distemper, hepatitis, parainfluenza, and parvovirus), and bordetella (kennel cough). You can expect most day cares to require dogs over 12 months to be spayed or neutered. Some will make exceptions, but that depends on the owner of the business. A good day care will want to know about any behavioral issues your dog has and will set up a trial to see if your dog is a good fit. This will usually begin with having your dog meet staff to determine how comfortable she is meeting and being handled by someone other than you. Assuming this goes well, they will go through whatever their preferred introduction method is. One day care we know has a kennel located adjacent to and in full view of the playroom. New dogs spend a half hour in that kennel before being admitted into the playroom. That way all the dogs, including the new kid, have a chance to understand that a newcomer has arrived. This sort of introduction is far more sensible than simply spinning the roulette wheel and seeing how your dog fares cold turkey in a new group.

We asked Suzanne Golter what behavioral benefit she has seen among her own clientele. She said, "Shy dogs become more confident. Under socialized dogs learn how to behave properly in a pack of dogs, including how to meet and greet other dogs and how to interpret social signals. Active dogs get their needs met, which means they are happier and healthier. And we have seen instances where dogs with separation anxiety get better over time."

There are plenty of benefits to your dog attending a well-run day care; dogs learn to play and interact in a healthy way that is safer if there is sufficient and well-trained staff to oversee the groups. While it can be expensive on a daily basis, taking advantage of it a couple times a week is doable for many and can help socialize your dog.

Dog Parks

Dog parks are the Mother of All Controversies among dog trainers. The average trainer truly hates them. Many say the dog park is akin to *Lord of the Flies*, a dystopian novel about how quickly civilized behavior can devolve into survival of the fittest. That's because some of our clients have had bad experiences that left psychological scars on them, or their dogs and we trainers are tasked with undoing the damage. Previously friendly dogs may have been attacked in a dog park and subsequently become nervous or fear aggressive near dogs. Yet for dog owners, especially

Although issues can arise in a dog park, many dogs and people depend on them as a fun social outlet.

those who live in a city, dog parks are a very tempting solution to help with exercise and socialization. At their best, they give dogs the chance to blow off steam in a fenced-in area and allow them to interact with other dogs. Dog parks are a little bit of a crapshoot, and if you are going to make use of them you need to have your eyes open and be aware of the risks. It is estimated that over 800 dog parks serve the 100 largest cities in the United States, and that doesn't take into account the hundreds or thousands in the suburbs and smaller cities. Increasingly, apartment complexes provide them for their residents' use.

Although dedicated dog parks may be something of an American phenomenon, informal gatherings of dogs and owners have taken place for decades in other countries. On a 2012 trip to Paris, Marc stumbled upon an impromptu dog park in the gardens directly behind the Louvre. Twenty-five or thirty owners turned their dogs loose in an unfenced area. The dogs played well, and none ran away. Although that might surprise the American reader, it will come as no shock to Parisians. Unlike in many parts of the United States, people bring their dogs everywhere in Paris, even to the outdoor cafes. The dogs become used to people and to one another. Interestingly, no one in Paris would ever think of accosting a dog owner asking to pet their dog or demanding to let their dogs "say hello." This just isn't done randomly as happens so frequently in the United States. Yet, by constantly exposing their dogs to city life, the dogs of Paris are remarkably well adjusted.

But sometimes things do go wrong in our dog parks. Recently we took an 8-month-old goldendoodle named Lizzy into our board and train program. Right away we noticed she was fearful around other dogs. When the owners took her out of the car, Lizzy saw several dogs walking past the parking lot. She frantically tried to pull her owner in the opposite direction.

"This is what I've been dealing with for the past 2 months," the owner said. "She tries to avoid other dogs at all costs. I feel so bad. She doesn't want to play anymore."

"Anymore?" we asked.

"Yes, she said, "Lizzy was a friendly puppy and we socialized her with a friend's dogs. But then we moved from the suburbs to the city. City life made her a little nervous, so we took her to the dog park to make new friends. She was timid at first, but the dogs were friendly, and they drew her out. She began to play with them, and I looked forward to taking her back. The next time we went, it was filled with different dogs, but Lizzy seemed happy, so I turned her loose. Things were going OK so when my phone rang, I took the call and got distracted. Before I knew it, I heard a scream and growling. I saw a much larger dog pinning Lizzy to the ground by her neck. I ran over, clapping my hands at the other dog trying to distract it. A random person—not even the dog's owner—helped me shoo the dog away. Lizzy wasn't badly hurt but she was shaking and whining so I took her right back home. Needless to say, that was the last time I took her to the dog park. Since then, Lizzy has been afraid of all other dogs, even little ones we pass during our walks. I feel so bad for her."

Because the authors are dog trainers, all too often we hear these stories from our clients. Perhaps our view of dog parks is skewed because people tend to tell us more about the problem encounters than the good times. But many idea-starved dog owners see things differently and, admittedly, have had mostly positive experiences. As one city dweller said to us recently, "I take Caesar to the park every day. It gives him the opportunity to burn off excess energy and helps keep me sane." What he didn't mention was that his dog was a 105-pound rottweiler. When we asked him if his dog had gotten into any scrapes there, he said rather matter-of-factly, "Oh, Caesar can

Fortunately, there is no bully in this group as introductions are made.

take care of himself"—the implication being that Caesar could take care of the other dogs as well!

This is precisely the point. For the majority of dog parks, as public spaces there is no reliable way of controlling who uses them. If a playground bully is throwing his or her weight around in dominant, over-aroused, and rude behavior, drama can quickly develop. Since most dog parks are unmonitored or supervised other than by owners, anything can happen, especially when owners become distracted or, worse yet, have a dog who can "take care of himself." Even if you have a tough dog, drama can develop with another large, unruly dog.

It is undeniable that many dogs thrive in the dog park and will never have anything more unpleasant to deal with than the average child will occasionally encounter on the playground. Those dogs often have a rowdy, bold style of play and they are not easily put off by a brief tiff. More sensitive dogs may do better with the dogs who are present one day, but not necessarily the next. And some dogs just don't seem to like dog parks as much as their owners who dreamed of using them to hang out with dog owners.

George Cockrell is a third-generation dog trainer in the Washington DC suburbs of Maryland. He reports that he often has the following conversation with clients:

Client: "My dog really doesn't do well at the dog park."

George: "Then don't go to the dog park."

Client: "But I want to go to the dog park!"

George: "Go ahead. Just leave the dog at home. He doesn't like it there."

Here's what we recommend. If you are familiar with your local dog park and the dogs who usually frequent it, make use of that park if your own dog plays well there. Avoid bringing favorite toys with you if your dog will object to sharing them. When you arrive at the park, *do not immediately go in through the gates.* We cannot stress this enough. Pause outside the fence and observe what is happening inside. Take 5 minutes to watch. Do you see happy dogs playing as you would want? Or do you see bullying and harassment? Is there humping, neck biting, or dogs being overwhelmed as we discussed earlier in this chapter? If so, walk away and turn the time into a nice neighborhood walk with no tension. But if the dogs are playing well and your dog wants to join, by all means, take your dog in.

Don't be nervous but remain vigilant and pay attention to your dog's play as well as to new dogs who may enter the park. Sometimes a new dog can destabilize a group that is playing well together. Be alert. Do talk to the other people there because they may know a lot about what dogs to watch out for. Plus, you can make

Although this incident ended peacefully, its best to interrupt such moments in dog play before one of the dogs takes offence.

new friends, too, but don't forget to keep an eye on not only your dog, but the overall picture. Sometimes a scuffle will start far from where your dog is playing, but natural curiosity can cause all the dogs to run into that situation to see what is happening. Nothing good can come from that. Finally, avoid taking tiny dogs into uncontrolled situations. All that being said, we are well aware that millions of dogs have excellent experiences at dog parks every day. We just want to arm you with information, so you have the best possible chance of enjoying way more good times than bad.

What to Do in Case of a Dogfight

Fortunately, serious dogfights are rare. More common are scuffles in which both dogs make a lot of scary noise, but each is hoping to get out of the situation, according to Chad Mackin, dog socialization expert and blogger at www.packtobasics.net. In these instances, he says, "Loud noises like from an air horn or water from a bucket or hose may distract them for the instant you need to separate them."

"The more committed the dogs are, however," he continued, "the more dangerous the fight. Though it is not always so, serious fights can be much quieter than a scuffle because each dog is focused on the other and doesn't waste energy on vocalizing threats. There is no *safe* way to break up a dog fight . . . though some methods are safer than others. This is why prevention is critical."

In our discussions with Mackin, he mentioned that in an emergency one person can grab the back legs of each dog and lift as high as they can, placing as much weight as possible on the front legs. Then walk backward, separating the dogs. Leash both dogs as soon as humanly possible so one doesn't flee only to have the other chase.

If one dog is latched onto the other, you may find it difficult to get him to let go. Rather than hitting the dog—which may not be effective anyway—insert a stout wooden dowl, rod, or stick into the jaws and rotate to pry them open. Then be prepared to have someone instantly move the other dog away while you leash the dog who had latched on.

CHAPTER 11

Playing with Your Aging Dog

There is something poignant and special about our old canine friends. Far quicker than we would want, they slow down, get stiffer, and sleep more deeply. We remember when we could not sneak into our own home without being greeted at the door by three eager dogs. When they were younger, they heard the car door before we even entered the house. Now we come home to find them oblivious, sleeping on dog beds. Yet their body clocks never fail to tell them when it's almost mealtime. Over the years, we have fallen into a comfortable routine with our older dogs, but it is one that, by necessity, must change gradually over time. We still want them to enjoy life, but we must take their age into account.

Dogs, just like humans, benefit from exercise—both mental and physical—as they age. But they mature faster than we do. That means adapting exercise and play may start earlier than we'd like it to, but our dogs' good life will continue as long as possible with proper adjustments. The idea that a dog ages 7 years for every one of ours is mythological, but it is certainly true they feel their age quicker than us. If there is one sadness inherent in our love affair with dogs, it is the all too short nature of it.

Yet we can extend the lives of our dogs and keep them happy as they age with good nutrition, regular veterinary care, and, critically, with play. We won't dwell on the tough parts of the canine relationship, or of the human experience. But you should take note that cognitive decline can indeed affect dogs, especially those who don't use their minds to solve behavioral puzzles and to explore the environment as much as they did when they were younger.

Your dog will likely enjoy better mental and physical health if you continue to engage his mind and body. Play is going to be an important part of that. But, before we continue, let's make a few assumptions for the purposes of this chapter:

- Your older dog is mobile.
- Your older dog is in reasonable health.
- Your older dog is as pain-free as you can help him to be.
- You know your older dog's stamina limitations.

If he has arthritis and doesn't want to move much, talk to your vet about treatment to mitigate pain. Signs of pain can include increasing difficulty with stairs, getting out of bed, standing up from the down position, as well as laying into the down position slowly, and decreased appetite. In many instances arthritic pain is treatable and many dogs will find relief from low grade chronic discomfort with a bit of veterinary and owner assistance. Remember that dogs can't complain and describe their symptoms to you. But you will notice slow and subtle shifts in his behavior. These are clues you should seek assistance to help him be more comfortable so he can also be more mobile and active into his later years.

Although medication may be indicated in certain cases, some veterinarians and owners have also found improvements with alternative therapies. Many of these techniques have been available to humans for hundreds or even thousands of years. Veterinarians in many states can now study and become licensed in doggy acupuncture, canine chiropractic, and massage. Holistic veterinarians receive additional training in Eastern medicine, including herbal and homeopathic approaches. Western medicine has only been around

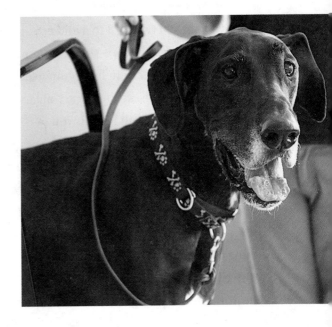

for a few hundred years, but Eastern medicine has been around for thousands. Finally, don't underestimate the importance of dental health. Tooth pain can cause your dog to stop eating and lose vitality. Infection under the gums can cause rapid disease of the blood, heart, and even eyes. Bad breath and brown buildup on teeth are not normal. So be sure to speak with your vet about the range of options if you suspect your dog has more than normal aches and pains.

Either way, knowing your dog and his physical limitations is important. We don't want to overtax him. If you sense he might injure himself playing a certain game, it is best to avoid that one and find a different way to interact with your dog. As an example, one of our own dogs has shown signs of stiffness, but we still play fetch with that dog. We adjust the distance that we throw, and we avoid throwing discs because dogs so often try to make quick twists to catch them. That's a common way for a more fragile dog to tear the ACL in his knee for example. So, we'll switch to a ball and just toss a bit shorter, being careful to avoid overly hot times of the day or slippery footing if it has rained or snowed.

Movement Is Life

We will help you try hard to avoid cognitive decline and muscle wasting, as these can cut your dog's lifetime short. He must do more than sleep. Even into his dotage, there is huge benefit to helping him use his brain and his body. And if you happen to be a senior citizen at the same time as your dog, walking and playing with him to keep him healthier will benefit you in the same ways. When humans feel pain, we tend to sit and rest more. Many older adults do this. But science has proven this can be a mistake that leads to an unfortunate cycle of decline. Resting too much leads to a sedentary lifestyle, which means we use our muscles less. Our muscles start to waste away and we may begin to gain weight, leading to yet more pain and more difficulty engaging in physical activities. Unfortunately, this can be a self-perpetuating cycle that may include decreasing brain activity. This can lead to faster cognitive decline. Studies show that older adults who live with a dog may live longer, healthier lives. We do not doubt it. How similar dogs and humans have become over the millennia! You can pay attention to any needed pain management and give your dog activities that will keep him sharp and stronger. The payoff is he'll stay happy and active for longer.

So, let's help your dog move and enjoy activities that engage his brain, his body, and which appeal to his instincts.

The first thing we recommend for the aging dog is an activity that we have suggested in every one of our books since we first began writing. Take your dog on one or two daily neighborhood walks. Games are important. Love and affection are part of the foundation. But walks are the simplest, easiest to do activity, one that your dog needs and which will keep him healthy longer.

Walks may get a bit harder as he gets older. He'll have less energy and won't move quite as fast as he used to. Maybe he'll get tired sooner. Take him out, nevertheless. Rather than reducing the frequency of your walks, just cut them a little shorter and keep him out of weather extremes. The reason we are so adamant about this is because . . .

. . . the walk exercises both the body and the mind.

While it is true that many aging dogs lose at least some of their hearing or sight, they still have their noses. Your older dog almost certainly retains his keen sense of smell. Puppies are born with ears sealed and eyes closed. They'll open their eyes about 10 days after birth. And their ear passages will open about a week later. In our long experience with dogs, one of the things we can assure you is that not only is your dog's nose his first sense—he almost immediately uses it to find its his mother's milk, but it is also a sense that he will keep for his entire lifetime.

Marc's rat terrier Scooter is 17.5 years old. Cataracts have dimmed her eyesight by 70 percent and old age has dimmed her hearing by about half. The rat terrier breed is a little hunting dog. Back in the 1930s through the 1950s, they were the

dog most commonly found on American farms, used to keep vermin out of barns and grain.

They owe their hunting expertise to an alert sense of hearing with oversize ears and a keen sense of smell. While Scooter's hearing may not be what it used to be, her sense of smell is still sharp. When Marc takes her out for a walk, she can sense exactly where she is based on the smell of the ground. She still loves to sniff around her Little Dog Farm and find something nasty to roll on. Scooter never fails to put her nose down and explore the scents of nature as much as she did at 3 years old.

Because she is partially blind, Marc whistles a specific tune when he puts her food down. Scooter comes around the corner into the kitchen, puts her nose down, and within a moment she finds her food each and every time.

Like Scooter, your old friend will still have his sense of smell. But here's where feeding Scooter gets even more interesting. Knowing that she can't easily see her bowl, Marc decided to pick her up and put her down right in front of it rather than have her find the food herself. It became immediately clear that Scooter didn't like that. When Marc first tried it, she walked away from the bowl after only a few bites. Scooter eats much better when she finds the food herself. She wants to use her nose. She needs the stimulation to her brain, and it affects her appetite. Even at her age, Marc finds she is happier if he continues to integrate Scooter's nose into the Find Your Dinner game. She does hear the special whistle, and when she scents her own way to the food, she usually eats all of it.

Walking your dog once or twice a day provides a similar benefit. All around us, especially outdoors, scent surrounds you and your dog in a large three-dimensional bubble. Air currents constantly change the sensory input. *We* don't generally notice anything other than a strong scent, such as when a neighbor grills a steak in a nearby yard. And we notice that only temporarily. But your dog notices everything, and we mean *everything*. This is why dogs can be trained to alert diabetics to high or low blood sugar because the scents of perspiration and breath change. Dogs have also been trained to detect drugs, bombs, track people and to identify specific diseases and biological agents. No matter how much his other senses may dim, his sense of smell is still powerful, and your walks give him much needed stimulation. He moves his body, which is valuable physical stimulation, and he uses a huge percentage of his brain by scenting the ground and air on his walk, which supplies critical mental stimulation.

Depending on age and mobility, you will need to alter the length and maybe even the speed of your walk. When your labrador, Doc, was 2 years old, you could walk him as fast, as far and as long as you wanted. Even if you took him on a 5-mile run, you might tire well before him. But when he's 10 years old, we recommend you take Doc on shorter walks, in the 20-minute vicinity. This is where knowing your dog and his physical condition can really help.

Remember to account for the weather, as your dog may not be able to handle extremes and will tire faster in the heat. As time goes on, older dogs also tend to become less sure-footed on ice or slippery ground. Some may even appreciate a coat or sweater.

Despite these precautions, your dog will continue to enjoy getting out, moving, and sniffing his route as he always done. Those walks give your dog a chance to strengthen his muscles and keep his mind active. That's because when he sniffs, he is actually accumulating and concentrating scent molecules, so the odor becomes stronger the longer he sniffs. To you it may look aimless, but he's analyzing something like this: "A mouse hid here, 4 hours ago. A female dog peed there. She's young, in good health, she's not in heat. She was with a person, 3 hours ago."

Using his senses this way will help your dog remain sharper than if he never gets out.

Keeping Those Old Tricks Alive

Years ago, you may have taught your dog a couple of tricks. Some of them may be harder to do now. If you taught him to roll over, he might find that difficult if he has become stiff. But he can still give paw, speak, and find his toy.

Consider asking your dog to do a trick before eating just as you used to. If he can't hear you as well, integrate hand signals into his tricks. You'll be surprised how quickly he'll pick up on your additional body language.

Marc's dog Gus became completely deaf at the age of 12, but Marc was able to communicate with him using hand signals Gus learned when he was only 1 year old. In his dotage, Gus would respond to the hand signals for come, sit, down, fetch, and more—this made life with an old dog lovely because the lines of communication remained completely open.

Marc fondly remembers occasions when he would have to run over to tap Gus on the shoulder so he would notice a signal. There was something very sweet about still communicating with him when the rest of his world went quiet. In fact, now 40 years later, that is exactly how Marc communicates with his dog Tippy, also mostly deaf with age. The more things change, dogs remain both constant and constantly with us.

Don't obsess about your dog's aging process. He doesn't dwell on it. He adapts and may even benefit from hidden blessings. For example, many dogs have had anxiety or stress at loud noises, like fireworks. Typically, their anxiety decreases or goes away altogether when they lose some of their hearing. The dimming of the sound to these dogs is the cloud with a silver lining. The Monks recall several of their German shepherds who would hide at the sound of thunderstorms but later in life didn't notice the boomers. Instead, they would happily chew a bone during evening recreation while lightning bolts lit the top of the mountain.

Opposite page: *Filling a toy with a smelly treat will engage even an older dog in a game of Find It.*

Find the Toy

Because the sense of smell remains, if you taught any of the rainy-day games in Chapter 5 (page 87) you can still use some of these to keep his mind working through mental puzzles. If you haven't yet, now is a perfect time. One of the best activities is find your toy. You can use one of his favorite playthings. Add a strong scent to it by rubbing a hot dog on it, or coat it with a bit of peanut butter, or use the strategy of cutting a slit in a tennis ball and fill it with treats so that there is a food scent. If your dog never especially liked toys before, you can either go through the process of experimenting to find one he responds to, or you can skip that step altogether and just hide a treat.

Of course, we recommend you keep an eye on him while playing with food scented toys because older dogs are just as inclined as always to chew a toy apart to get the treats. If that's a concern, you'll find a number of "smart toys" designed to hold food like a puzzle while your dog works out how to safely extract tidbits. But it is healthy to engage your dog's mind in problem solving. The act of working through a canine version of the Rubik's Cube activates your dog's mind, helping him stay cognitively sharp for longer.

Very early in this book, we stated that dogs are complex, problem-solving domes-ticated predators, and we stand by that statement. Once you learn to appeal to his nature, you'll see how giving your older dog behavioral puzzles to solve will keep him engaged with you and with life.

Younger and Older Dog Interactions

Marc and the Monks have been training dogs for a long time, and often see clients more than once. A common time to see a client a second time is when their first dog is older and they have acquired a second dog as a friend for the first.

This can be a great way to keep a maturing dog feeling younger longer.

It's better to add a younger dog or puppy when your first is still spry enough to have fun with a newcomer. It is not ideal to add a new dog if your oldest and best

The older dog doesn't want the puppy right in her face so she turns her head away as a signal.

Although the puppy remains playful, she took the hint and moved away—just enough.

friend is unable to play with or enjoy a friend. But many older dogs in reasonable health enjoy having a puppy around to socialize with. Just like humans, it helps them feel younger because it gives them something interesting to see and do, providing valuable psychological and physical nourishment.

Your older dog may help the younger learn some of the rules and behavior the new kid will need to be a good member of the household as well. You still need to train your puppy, of course, since your nonverbal dog can't be expected to teach commands or take on a disciplinary role, but your older dog can model better behaviors for your young dog, and make sure that it learns how to interact with humans and peers. Dogs often mirror one another, so yes, there is a good chance that if you take an active role, your older fellow can help educate his new pal. But don't make him do all the heavy lifting by himself. A younger pup with excess energy can overpower an older dog and we'll want to help him avoid strains or injury.

Remember we recommend keeping a new dog on the leash in the home for the initial 2 weeks as we discussed in Chapter 10 (page 177). That leash or drag line is going to help you pull the puppy out of your older dog's face if he gets too pushy. No one wants to be jumped on while they're napping. You don't like it, and neither will the old man.

Puppies are filled with boundless energy and may politely entice your dog to play, but they may also become more insistent than the old dog can easily tolerate. Although your first dog can help educate your second dog, it is not his responsibility to teach all the rules of civilized behavior to your puppy. That's your job. So, if you see the puppy begin to behave inappropriately, pull him off gently but insistently to give your old guy a break.

There is nothing wrong with periodically crating your new kid with a bone to give your old dog this respite. Carefully curate their play, so that your old dog is not overwhelmed. If you manage the first few weeks of interaction carefully, you'll likely find them forming a close bond as they become packmates. Your older dog will probably kick up his heels in ways that he may not have done in years. You can absolutely see your dog perk up and play more than he has in years when you've introduced a new puppy. But we want to make sure your dog isn't being faced with contact sports.

One of our clients told us about a game that naturally developed with her younger and older dog. She sat in a circle with both dogs, and often another family member, to play a game she named "push." They easily taught the older dog to push a soft ball to them with her nose and then the humans would push it back. The older dog loved this game. With time and by observation, the younger dog learned how to play as well. The people named the ball "the indoor ball." Push became a popular game in the home. In fact, sometimes the dogs initiated it by bringing the indoor ball to the owners, and it allowed the older dog to play while lying comfortably on the floor.

Generous use of the crate and crate training will also help that relationship build into a strong bond as your new dog will have a private place to relax, chew a bone and stay out of your other dog's hair.

A final word on adding the second dog to a formerly one-dog home. Your first guy is used to being an only child. He's had you and your environment to himself. And you are not used to thinking about apportioning and supervising resources that are naturally valuable to dogs. It is advisable to, at least temporarily, put away high-value goodies such as rawhide and bones, including any favorite toy that may cause your original dog to become possessive. Some dogs are good sharers, but not all, and we want to help build a healthy relationship rather than a competitive or possessive one. We wrote about this extensively in our book, *Let Dogs Be Dogs*. There is a lot to know about the

multiple-dog household. But perhaps the most important thing is that, overseen by a knowledgeable owner, a new companion can help breathe new life into your old friend.

Swimming and Hydrotherapy

Many of our us live or vacation near water. Some have beach or lake houses or even have a swimming pool. Just like humans who find that moving in water is good low-impact exercise that reduces pressure on joints, swimming and hydrotherapy are good for most aging dogs if taught with care.

Even if you live hundreds of miles from the nearest body of water and you don't have a swimming pool, chances are good that you'll find a vet-approved hydrotherapy location near you. Also, doggy day cares are increasingly adding swimming or hydrotherapy to their list of services.

We will tell you two ways that hydrotherapy is taught to dogs but keep in mind that there are many approaches. Your dog may already be a knowledgeable swimmer, but if he has never been in the water before, you're going to want to teach this slowly with the assistance of a professional.

One hydrotherapy machine consists of a large tank of soothing warm water. The floor of the tank is actually a treadmill belt. The dog is helped into the machine while the belt is turned off. The water only comes up to his hips so he won't worry, and he may wear a harness to help him stay centered. Once he gets used to this contraption, the belt is turned on so that the dog is walking slowly in the water. Over time as he gets used to it, and depending on your dog, the therapist may recommend increasing speed to a fast walk or eventually, a slow trot.

This is incredibly effective, low-impact exercise intended to halt or even reverse weakness from the muscle wasting that creeps up on so many older dogs. Our friend Patrick noticed his rottweiler mix, Trixie, slowing down a great deal at the age of 9. His vet recommended hydrotherapy, as we've just described. Patrick was skeptical at first, unsure whether he was simply being upsold. But he quickly found that not only did Trixie become stronger, regaining a good measure of her former vigor, but that she also looked visibly happy when she knew it was hydrotherapy time.

Although it is good for dogs, this form of therapy must be overseen by someone who really knows what they're doing. On the other hand, if your dog has been swimming in your pool all his life, feel free to continue. Just remember that he may tire out much faster than before. If you have not previously added a dog swimming pool ramp, consider doing that now. It's an easy add-on that can help your dog get in and out of the pool and prevent an emergency. You'll also find a full array of dog life vests if you go boating or swimming with your dog. We like swimming and water sports for dogs . . . under careful supervision.

Many people teach their young dogs to swim at a beach or a lake wearing a long 15- or 20-foot leash. Your older dog may not have needed a line for years, but he may need it now. If the tide pulls him out or his attention starts to wander, he can find himself in trouble and too tired to swim himself out of it. So, keep a line on him, if necessary, but water has brought many an old dog back to life for additional and enjoyable years.

Our Responsibilities as Dog Owners

We love our dogs. Taking on a dog means taking on a responsibility to keep your dog as physically and mentally healthy as possible so she can enjoy the longest and fullest life possible with you. That responsibility doesn't end just because your dog has become older. If anything, an old dog needs you more than ever to extend her lifespan through activities that strengthen her mind and body.

No one knows you better than the dog with whom you have shared hearth and home. You've studied one another's habits and fit one another like a comfortably broken-in pair of shoes. Older dog trainers, like your authors, have our favorite leashes. Some of them are 30 years old. We are attached to them, thinking back about all the dogs we worked with using that tool. Although we, too, may have a melancholy or sentimental moment thinking about our old guys as they become grayer and stiffer, we try to learn from our dog friends. If we listen, they can teach us the art of aging gracefully. Our job is to help them extract every joyful moment life has to offer. And we can indeed do that with the assistance of purposeful play.

EPILOGUE

Dogs remind us of a fundamental wisdom that often eludes us in our self-preoccupation. More than anything else, dogs are creatures of play, whose spontaneous interaction with life bespeaks its goodness.
—The Monks of New Skete

Chances are that as a child, the first time you met a dog, you were transfixed from the moment your eyes met. Even babies will reach out a hand to puppies and dogs. We instinctively want to touch them. And unlike most of the animal kingdom, they not only want our touch, they crave it and will seek it out. An online magazine surveyed over 11,000 parents asking what their baby's first word was. Of the 15 most common answers, "dog" or "doggy" came in fifth place, well ahead of words for grandparents.[1]

Our friends Patrick and Uriel have a son named Caleb. Now a little more than two, Caleb delights in helping to hold the leash to walk their dog Molly, a chihuahua mix. We had the pleasure to witness Caleb's infant fascination with Molly grow from staring to reaching out and touching her. As he got a little older, Caleb learned eye-to-hand coordination in part from wanting to hold a ball he could drop for Emma, the other family dog who loves to retrieve anything he drops. Caleb is old enough to toss the ball now. He and Emma never tire of the game.

Not everyone is lucky enough to grow up with a dog from infancy. Neither of your authors did, although we were each fortunate enough to have a family dog later during childhood. The impact has been indelible on both of us. Brother Christopher

---

1   www.popsugar.com/family/Most-Common-First-Words-According-Moms-27331155.

fondly remembers putting on big gloves and playing with Deenie, a toy Manchester terrier who would pretend to bite at the gloves. Marc threw fallen apples from a big tree for Gus to run after and fetch, returning them with juice dribbling down his chin. Both of us grew up playing with our dogs because they were our best friends, because we were children and children want someone to play with. As for our dogs, they wanted to play, too, because it is in the nature of a dog to express his joy of life at every possible moment. Neither of your authors thought about what we were teaching our dogs as we played. And neither do most people who grow up with a dog. We didn't always teach them the right lesson through our games. But like all people, our dogs brought us joy through good times and bad. For people, some days may be better than others, and although that may also be true of dogs, they sure do have more good days, especially when they have someone who will play with them.

As we have grown older, living with and loving multiple generations of dogs, we've noticed and been fascinated by the way even our senior and elderly dogs accept and adapt to the changes time has bestowed on them. And in some sense, we seem to keep each other feeling younger longer. The dog will always want to go out to smell the proverbial roses. That is her gift. She will never tire of the wonders that life offers the living. Dogs are so connected to and involved with the present moment that they would not likely dwell on mortality were they able.

Isn't it their love of life itself that draws us so strongly to dogs? Are they not fully alive, endowed with a vitality unencumbered by worry and fear? The dog expresses his nature through fidelity and play. He is loyal, cleaving to those he loves, and even as an elderly dog, he wants to pick up the occasional stick, roll on the ground or kick up his heels to run a few steps before he tires. By indulging him in play and the daily outing, we ourselves participate more fully in life, connecting back to the natural world. The dog pulls our head out of emails and smart phones, demanding that we see and share in his pleasures and his observations. *Squirrel! Another dog! Children!*

We have a confession to make that is probably obvious by now. We sowed nuggets of dog behavior improvements throughout the games in this book much the way people who cook for children often hide vegetables in a recipe. It's a given that dogs want to play so the only question is: what will the play teach them? With learning-based games and activities we can engage a dog to the point where she will willingly volunteer for most of the behaviors we could ever ask of a dog:

- Let me clip your nails.
- Potty in the right place.
- Tell me when you have to go out.
- Come when called.
- Get your ball and bring it back.
- Go to your bed.
- Play nicely with other dogs.
- And maybe most important of all, know how and when to calm yourself down and relax with me.

Dogs play focused on the joy of now without thinking about yesterday or worrying about tomorrow.—Marc Goldberg

That is a partial list of what we covered here; each nugget of good behavior hidden in a game the same way peas and carrots hide under a layer of beef and mashed potatoes in shepherd's pie. Dogs bring a certain joy of life, a *joie de'vivre,* to all who live with them and who are open to communicating with them and teaching them. And although this book has focused on teaching you how to play with your dog, we deeply believe the ultimate beneficiary will be the relationship between you both. And that is because life with a dog means you'll never have to play solitaire.

ACKNOWLEDGMENTS

What a pleasure and honor is has been for us to write this third book together as coauthors and friends. From decades of training dogs in our boarding school programs—the Monks of New Skete in Cambridge, New York, and Marc Goldberg in suburban Chicago—we have learned that the dog is at the emotional center of the home.

With our agent, Kate Hartson, and photographer, Vincent Remini, we function like a literary family. Their assistance has been invaluable. If Kate were a dog, she would be a German Shepherd, protectively herding us always toward a better book. Of course, agents want their clients to succeed, but Kate's approach to our dog books is on a higher level, curating photographs and chapters from outline through writing to photoshoot. A charter member of the canine paparazzi, Vincent will lay down in a field of wet grass and belly-crawl to photograph a litter of puppies as they scatter like cats. Vincent traveled thousands of miles to capture the beautiful images of dogs and people you've enjoyed in this book. We are truly fortunate and grateful to have this team by our side and we look forward to future projects together.

Our editor, Ann Treistman, is a dog lover and a highly experienced editor who brings a keen eye for making our books both beautiful and better written. Like a terrier digging for the bone, she has tenaciously uncovered the best vision for this book. We are indeed fortunate to work with her and this book certainly reflects that.

Friends shared their thoughts about our work, and we owe them thanks: Valerie Erwin, for help with agility photography; Mary Mazzeri; Martin Deeley; Chad Mackin; Cyndy Douan; George Cockrell; Suzanne Golter; and in memory of Pat Trichter.

Through the International Association of Canine Professionals we have met some of the finest trainers in the world. Visit them at CanineProfessionals.com.

Special thanks to the New Skete community of monks, nuns, and lay people, as well as Aaron Pfeiffer and Patrick Farrell. Sincere thanks to the many people and dogs who allowed us into their lives to photograph *The Joy of Playing with Your Dog.*

INDEX

ABOUT THE AUTHORS

The Monks of New Skete have been breeding and raising German shepherds, as well as training dogs of all breeds for more than 40 years. They are the authors of *The Art of Raising a Puppy, How to Be Your Dog's Best Friend*, and more. Their books have sold a combined total of over 1.5 million copies. The monks note, "For many of us, love for creation deepens through the relationships we form with our pets, particularly our dogs."

The monks' relationship with dogs began in the early days of the monastery when they were given a German shepherd named Kyr. He quickly became a beloved pet who led the monks to adopt more German shepherds. Eventually, at the request of friends, they began breeding these beautiful and intelligent animals. They wrote their first bestseller at the request of a dog training client who was also a book editor. No one was more surprised at their eventual celebrity than the monks. The New Skete Monastery is located in Cambridge, New York. Visit the monks at newskete.org.

Marc Goldberg has been training dogs since he was a child. Winning multiple AKC obedience competitions early on gave him a quick start, but he was eventually to find more satisfaction in helping others enjoy their dogs than in winning trophies. Now Marc is a nationally renowned dog trainer and former president of the International Association of Canine Professionals. He often trains dogs and writes books with the Monks of New Skete. Marc is based near Chicago, Illinois, training for clients at his Little Dog Farm. He lives with his partner and their three beloved dogs: Scooter, a rat terrier; Tippy, a border collie mix; and Friday, a German shepherd. Visit Marc at chicagodogtrainer.com and marcgoldbergdogtrainer.com.

Together, the authors have written three books including *Let Dogs Be Dogs* and *The Art of Training Your Dog*. They teach seminars featuring their dog training method. The seminars are popular with dog owners and trainers alike. Learn more at theartoftrainingyourdog.com.